12 PRINCIPLES TO MAKE YOUR LIFE EXTRAORDINARY
Copyright © 2017 - E. W. Jackson, Sr.
Published by STAND Foundation, Inc.
Chesapeake, VA 23328

www.STANDAmerica.us
EWJackson.com

ISBN-13: 978-0-692-86324-4

Cover design by Rakiyt Zakari
Book layout by Tara Billups Haynes

Printed in the United States of America

12

PRINCIPLES

to MAKE YOUR

LIFE

EXTRAORDINARY

E.W. JACKSON

Dedicated to my Lord and Savior Jesus Christ.
May He be pleased with it.

Table of Contents

INTRODUCTION

The original version of this book was written nine years ago. It has undergone such extensive revision and so much additional material has been added, that the title and chapter headings have also been changed. For all intents and purposes, it is a new book based on many of the same ideas but informed by nine years of experience since I wrote the first version. I've added two new chapters that arguably are the most important in the book.

Life is an unending process of growth, or it should be. One of my greatest learning experiences in the years since the first publication was running for Lt. Governor of Virginia. Winning the nomination of my party and nearly a million votes was part of the extraordinary life God has given me. This book became an issue in that campaign. It was written to a Christian audience, but some of the reporters committed to stopping me had no Christian frame of reference. I was amazed by the torturous interpretations they put on some of my words. However, the point of the book is that if you practice these principles, you cannot be stopped. You can be attacked, even wounded, but "this is the victory that has overcome the world – our faith." John 5:4

Every human being has a destiny. That is not to imply some climactic end which puts the exclamation point on your life. Nor is it a mechanistic framework to which you are bound so that no matter what you do, you cannot escape that preordained blue print. I believe that you and I were created by the Almighty, omniscient, omnipresent God who loves us with infinite love. Within the framework of His moral law, He wants us to be happy and fulfilled.

By His grace we can overcome the wounds of life - bad experiences, bad parents, bad people and our own mistakes. The scars of life become part of the beautiful mosaic that makes us who we are. Instead of hopelessness and despair, life should be filled with inspiration and purpose. Your destiny is to reach the highest and best life to which your character, skills and abilities can take you. What life has for you is based on what God has in you. What is planned for you is based on what God put in you Your unique design presages your specific purpose.

There are many people who will tell you how to fulfill your destiny without God. I am telling you that it cannot be done. I will even go beyond that. You cannot live the satisfying and fulfilling life that is your heritage unless you submit yourself – spirit, soul and body - to Jesus Christ as your Savior and Lord.

Since the first book was published, I have encountered many people who told me that it had such a profound impact on their lives that they read it three or more times. It is my hope that this new version will have an even more significant and positive impact on the lives of those who read it. It is still a Christian book, written for Christian people, but of course I hope that those who are not Christians will read it and experience changed lives.

I learned the hard lesson through my political campaign experience that reporters will read it without a biblical frame of reference and twist my words into something I never intended. Some of the twisting was manifestly dishonest, hoping to sabotage my candidacy. However, I have tried to anticipate the possibility of honest misunderstanding by being more clear wherever it seemed necessary.

Honest readers will find that both versions were written to help Christians find and fulfill their God given calling and destiny. Neither book was written as a polemic against anything or anyone except a wasted life. These books were written to help people, not hurt them. I want every one of you to live an extraordinary life. When you stand before God, I want Him to say, "well done." If one word in these books contributes to that outcome, I will consider it an extraordinary success.

1

1ST PRINCIPLE

"Believe It"

True faith, the faith that God imparts to us as we seek Him, is not merely an attitude that allows us to endure life's hardships. It is not positive thinking, although there is nothing wrong with thinking in a positive way. As a general proposition, positive thinking is definitely better than negative thinking.

True faith is not holding fast to a set of doctrines. Islamic terrorists do that, but they do not have true faith. (Of course the "god" of Islam is not the God of the Bible, contrary to what is widely promoted.) A person who has faith should certainly hold fast to a set of principles, but they have to be the right principles. Even that is not faith, but rather the outward behavior that a person of faith demonstrates. A true understanding of faith can only be found in the Bible. Biblical faith is not simply accepting things as they are. It is the power to change things into what they should be, what God wants them to be.

Biblical faith is being fully persuaded that every Word God says in the Scriptures in true. When every fiber of your being believes God's Word and believes that you have what it says you have and can do what it says you can do, you not only have faith, but faith has you.

Faith is not a head thing, but a heart thing. Nevertheless, it must infuse your mind, will and emotions - every fiber of your being.

Let me use an illustration familiar to us all. While I do not play the lottery and recommend strongly against it, we have all seen the news of lottery winners. Some people with very little money win vast sums, hundreds of millions of dollars. When a person wins the lottery, the gladness does not come when the money is in the bank. The moment a person confirms the winning ticket, before a single dollar has changed hands, there is happiness probably unlike anything he or she has ever known.

That's what true faith is like. It is knowing in a deep way that what you believe will happen, has is fact already happened, such that your entire being responds before there is any physical confirmation. You know you have the lottery money before you actually have a dime of it in the bank. Once you have confirmed that you have the winning ticket, you trust the lottery system to give you what it has promised. Faith in God, which is far better than playing and winning the lottery, is trusting Him to produce what He has promised.

With that kind of faith, you've already hit the lottery, and it's not a gamble. Faith in God is a sure thing when that faith is based on what the Word of God says. When someone knows they hit the lottery, they don't say, "I hope I get that money one day." No! They are already celebrating. They say, "I'm rich. They call Mom and Dad, brother, sister, friends and tell them.

They don't actually have physical possession of it, and yet they are convinced that it is theirs. That's faith. That's how you know you really believe. Your whole being scintillates with it although you have not seen or held it. You don't sit around worrying. When somebody calls to ask how you are doing, you don't complain. You rejoice for what is coming your way because in your mind you already have it, and your emotions reflect that.

The greatest expert on faith who ever lived, Jesus Christ, said, "All things, whatever you are praying and asking for, be believing that you received them, and they shall be yours." Mark 11:24 (Kenneth Wuest Expanded Translation, Grk N.T.) If you ever expect to go beyond where you are, your inner reality must reflect things as you want them to be, not as they are. Many Christians do not understand this. If you are not smiling, happy and at peace, you don't really believe you have it.

Abraham was a man of faith. He was good enough at to be commended by God and called the father of faith. (Rom.4:16) The key to Abraham's faith is found in his acceptance of the new name God gave him. When he was ninety nine years old, God changed his name from Abram, "father of lights," which referred to pagan religious practices, to Abraham, which means "father of (many) nations." His wife Sarah was ninety. He was so old that he considered his sexual life over and his wife had been barren all her life. It was a supreme act of faith for

Abraham to accept a covenant with God which promised a child. Abraham believed God and called "…those things that do not exist as though they did." (Romans 4:17)

There was a famine in Israel during the days of Elijah because there was no rain. Elijah was fed by ravens at the Brook of Cherith, but the Brook dried up. Then he was fed by a widow in a place called Zarephath when God miraculously multiplied her oil and meal to provide food until the rains began to fall and the earth yielded fruit again. When God was ready to end the famine, Elijah went up to the top of Mount Carmel to pray. He would pray a while and look up, pray a while and look up. After each time he prayed, he told his servant, "go look toward the sea." He did that seven times. On the seventh time, Elijah's servant came back and said, "There is a cloud, as small as a man's hand, rising out of the sea." (1 Kings 17 & 18)

What we may not realize is that before Elijah ever prayed for rain, he told King Ahab, you better go home and get some food, because "there is the sound of abundance of rain." Before a cloud ever appeared in the sky, Elijah heard the rain. Before a drop ever fell, Elijah heard the rain. Before there was the smell of moisture in the air, Elijah heard the rain.

Real faith, Biblical faith, the kind of faith Jesus was talking about is when you hear it before it happens; when you see it before it appears; when you feel it before it manifests; when you can touch it before it is tangible. Therefore, the faith question to you is: Do you hear it?

Do you see it? Do you feel it? Do you believe that you've already received it? Are you already celebrating? Are you already rejoicing?

Whatmountainsareyoufacinginyourlife?Jesus said,"… [W]hoever says to this mountain, 'Be removed and be cast into the sea,' and does not doubt in his heart, but believes that those things he says will be done, he will have whatever he says." (Mark 11:23) You may be thinking that you cannot convince yourself that you have what you in fact do not have. A young man once found an older and very successful man fishing at the same spot. The young man thought to himself, "This is my chance. I am going to pick his brain and learn all his secrets of success. He approached the older man respectfully and said to him, "Sir, I know that you have been extremely successful. Would you please share with me the secret of your success? For I too want to be successful. The old man looked at him intently, and beckoned him to come closer.

When the young man came within reach, he grabbed him and pushed his head under water at the bank of the river and held him there. After a few seconds he let him up to breath. As soon as the young man took a breath, he pushed his head under water again. He did that several times. Finally he was holding his head under water for so long that the young man was panic stricken thinking, "Surely I will drown." Just as he thought his lungs would soon be filled with water, the man pulled him out. After the young inquirer caught his breath, he asked the man angrily, "Why did you do that?" The old man said to him calmly, "When you want to succeed as badly as you wanted that last breath, you will."

The question is "How badly do you want it?" If you want the kind of success that is built upon eternal laws and principles of God, which cannot fail, then make a quality decision to believe the Word of God, not argue with it. Ask God to instill in you a hunger for the truth. I cannot make it happen for you. I can only offer you the truths that changed my life.

How can I be so sure it will work for you? Because the definition of truth is that it works all the time. It is eternal and without partiality. If these principles have worked for me and countless others, they will work for you. The more you practice them, the more you will see the evidence of their power in your life. They work! Now you must put them to work! Life has a way of causing us to drift and lose focus. Do not allow that to happen.

Be Patient

Hebrews 10:36 says, "For you have need of steadfast patience and endurance, so that you may perform and fully accomplish the will of God, and thus receive and carry away [and enjoy to the full] what is promised."(Amplified Version)

There will always be the temptation to quit when difficulties arise or you don't see quick results. When you stop believing and start doubting and making excuses, you kill the supernatural seed of faith that is working in your life, and drive a stake through the heart of your dreams.

Back in early 1980's I licensed a young man in the ministry. He married shortly after we met. He and his wife wanted children, but something was wrong. Try as they might, she could not get pregnant. In year one they had no children, nor in year two, three or four. Five, ten, fifteen years went by. Friends and family told them to adopt or try some artificial means. They refused to listen, but instead staked their faith on Psalm 127:3, which says, "Behold, children are a heritage from the Lord. The fruit of the womb is a reward."

This couple took the view that they had a promise from God, a "heritage" which included children, and that they would not believe anything else. One Sunday morning during their seventeenth year of marriage they walked into Church and announced that the wife was pregnant. They now have a beautiful daughter who has grown into an elegant Christian woman.

During that long period of waiting they had plenty of opportunities to stop believing. They could have become depressed and discouraged. They could have despaired of ever having children. They could have given up. They resisted those temptations and in the process learned how to respond with power in the face of adverse circumstances. Never lower your expectations to conform to your experience. Believe until your experience conforms to your expectations. It will happen.

Embrace Truth

In Mark 4:3-9, Jesus teaches an interesting truth: "Listen! Behold, a sower went out to sow. And it happened, as he sowed, that some seed fell by the wayside; and the birds of the air came and devoured it. Some fell on stony ground, where it did not have much earth; and immediately it sprang up because it had no depth of earth. But when the sun was up it was scorched, and because it had no root it withered away. And some seed fell among thorns; and the thorns grew up and choked it, and it yielded no crop. But other seed fell on good ground and yielded a crop that sprang up, increased and produced: some thirty-fold, some sixty, and some a hundred." And He said to them, "He who has ears to hear, let him hear!"

The seed Jesus talks about in this parable is the Word of God. When that Word is spoken into the life of a human being, it is supernatural seed, packed with power to produce the promise it contains. For example everything written in this book is to help you understand the truth and believe it, but you must choose your response. That is what the parable is about.

You can hear truth which calls you to a higher level of life, but you can allow that truth to go in one ear and out of the other. That is seed that falls by the wayside.

Or you may think about it, but that's all. You soon forget, and it never has an impact on your life. You are too busy "living." That is seed which falls on stony ground. Then some people may hear truth and become very excited about it. They might even make a decision to change their lives as a result of the truth they have heard. Yet they soon find that their problems, responsibilities or associations with people who want them to stay on their mundane level cause them to forget what they were once so excited about. That seed fell among thorns. Then there are those who hear truth, allow it to sink into their hearts, and change the way they think and act. They hold fast to it and never let go. Soon their lives are transformed, and they never look back.

If you are not receiving seed into good ground, it cannot produce fruit in your life. For example if someone is struggling with an addiction such as smoking, drinking or even drugs, faith can rid them of it. What most people do is try to use will power, which is usually too weak to resist the physical and mental craving of addiction. They are trying to stop a bad tree from yielding bad fruit by cutting off a branch instead of digging up the root. Before you know it they are right back where they started.

In order for you to reap good fruit, you must sow good seed. You are only going to reap what you sow. "Do not be deceived. God is not mocked; for whatever a man sows, that he will also reap." (Galatians 6:7). You must let God's promises take root in your life. This must be your attitude and your stand: "I don't care what the circumstances look like. My life will not be governed by circumstances, but by faith in God and His Word.

Jesus made faith unequivocal: "If you abide in Me, and my words abide in you, you will ask what you desire, and it shall be done for you." (John 15:7) Never allow people to kill your faith by making you feel guilty about wanting good things for yourself and others. It is not wrong to want good things in life. It is wrong to be selfish and self-centered. It is wrong to put things before God and people. We must have giving hearts, and share our good things with others. We use things to serve people, but never use people to get things.

Do not think that because God is merciful and kind, you are going to automatically get the best in life. That is not the way God works. You must have faith and put that faith to work for what you desire. The book of James says, "If any of you lacks wisdom, let him ask of God, who gives to all liberally and without reproach, and it will be given to him. But let him ask in faith, with no doubting, for he who doubts is like a wave of the sea driven and tossed by the wind. For let not that man suppose that he will receive anything from the Lord; he is a double-minded man, unstable in all his ways." (James 1:5-8)

One of the biggest lies ever told about faith is that God is going to do whatever He is going to do, and there is nothing we can do to change that. First of all, that is fatalistic thinking which posits that everything that happens is somehow God's will. That view is completely inconsistent with what the Bible teaches.

One of the many wonderful and instructive incidents which took place during Jesus' earthly ministry involved a woman who had been sick with an issue of blood for twelve years. She was ceremonially unclean according to

Jewish law and should not have even been out in public. In her unclean condition she had to face the question put to you earlier: How much do you want it? She believed in her healing enough that she was willing to take the risk in order to obtain it. She said to herself, "If only I may touch his garment, I shall be made well." (Matthew 9:21)

She fought her way through a thronging crowd which could have crushed her in their excitement to get close to the Celebrity Preacher. She came crawling up behind Him to grab His clothes. When she did, just as she had confessed, power flowed out of Him and she was healed immediately. With all the people grabbing him in the crowd, Jesus said, "Who touched my clothes?" But his disciples said to Him, "You see the multitude thronging You, and You say, 'Who touched Me?'" The difference between this woman and the crowd was that she touched him in faith, believing that the moment she put her hands on His clothes, she would be healed. And she was. When she told Him what she had done, He told her, "Daughter, your faith has made you well." (Mark 5:34)

This woman had tried everything. She was bankrupt, desperate and at the end of her rope. Before she grabbed Jesus garment, she grabbed hold of faith. As a result she drew on power that she had never known before. I guarantee you that her life was never the same. The faith that healed her of what had been incurable could meet every other need in her life whether financial, social or emotional.

What if she had never left her home? What if she had

never crawled through that crowd? What if she had never become convinced that touching His garment would bring the healing she sought. This woman was rewarded for her aggressive pursuit of what she wanted. She did not sit at home saying, "If God wants me healed, He will do it when He's ready." Instead she reached out for her healing and literally took hold of the love and power of God. Jesus affirmed her determination when He said to her, "'Be of good cheer, daughter; your faith has made you well.' And the woman was made well from that hour." Matthew 9:22

That same power is available to you today. Do you want a transformed life badly enough to believe, despite everything around you? If you do, the trajectory of your life will change. Stop allowing your dreams go up in smoke. Your faith can transform your whole life for the better. Your life can be extraordinary through the power of God.

Faith: The Invisible Substance

Everyone has areas of life which need dramatic change, but sometimes we beat our heads against a brick wall with little or no results. There is an easier and more effective way.

The Bible says, "faith is the substance of things hoped for, the evidence of things not seen." (Hebrews 11:1). The word "substance" is the Greek word "hupostasis," which literally means "that which stands under". In other words, faith is the foundation upon which our hopes rest. One translation says, faith is the "reality" of things hoped for.

It is also the evidence of things unseen. Evidence is usually seen after the fact as proof of what happened. It allows us to reach a conclusion, a verdict, without having been witnesses to the actual incident. For our purposes, it is the sealed proof that what you believe will indeed happen. This is the key to understanding creation. All visible things were born of the invisible. The creation of the life you desire to see begins with what you cannot see. It begins with faith.

We access that unseen power by faith. Everything your physical eye can see, your hand can touch, everything made by God or man, began in the invisible realm of the heart and mind. Everything we see began in the imagination of God or man. In other words, it began as something invisible.

That invisible power which God used to create all things, including you and me, was released by speaking His Word. You and I are made in the image and likeness of God. Faith connects us to the creative power of God Himself! This is the key to an extraordinary life.

It is true that "faith without works is dead." (James 2:26) It is also true that work without faith will make you dead. It will kill you; and yet this is how most people try to build success. We work ourselves to death with two, three or even four jobs trying to become financially secure. The result is high blood pressure, heart attacks, strokes, broken marriages, unhappy homes and a host of stress related problems. That is not how God designed us to function, and that way of life is doomed to create as many problems as it solves. I am not denigrating hard work. I still work long hours and often seven days a week. That is not how I live, just what I do. I've learned however that I cannot do what I do in my own strength. I must lean on and rely on God to guide and strengthen me. I've tried it the other way and I'll tell you that story later in the book.

God gave Adam the Garden of Eden and told him to tend it and dress it. Anyone who has ever tended a garden knows that it is a great deal of work. Keep in mind that Eden was not a small front yard, and Adam had no servants or assistants. Yet it was not until Adam sinned that God said to Adam, "In toil you shall eat…all the days of your life. In the sweat of your face you shall eat bread till you return to the ground." (Gen.3:17,19) "Toil" did not come into play until sin entered the picture.

Prior to that, Adam tended the Garden of Eden by faith, using the creative power of God. He was not striving, struggling and sweating. That did not come until after he disconnected from God. Your creative power is not in the sweat of your brow, but in your faith. That's why Christ said, "Come to me, all you who labor and are heavy laden, and I will give you rest. Take My yoke upon you and learn from Me…and you will find rest for your souls. For My yoke is easy and My burden is light." (Matthew 11:28-30)

When Jesus was asked, "What shall we do, that we may work the works of God?" He answered, "This is the

work of God, that you believe in Him whom He sent."
(John 6:29)

Who and what do you believe? Everyone has faith.
The question is, "faith in what?" You are operating your
life on the basis of a set of beliefs. Are they the right ones?
Believing the way God wants you to believe means being
grounded in the Word of God. To experience its awesome,
transforming power, you must believe it against all
circumstances and situations. No matter what else seems
to be happening around you.

God says He will prosper you. Believe that in the face
overwhelming financial hardship, and you will prosper.
God says He has healed you. Believe that when every fiber
of your being screams sickness, and you will be well. God
says He will deliver you from trouble. Believe that even
if trouble seems to overwhelm you like a tidal wave, and
help will come. Do not listen to friends, doctors, lawyers
or anyone else who tells you that faith will not work.
Believe what God says. He will never fail you. Mountains
must move when they encounter faith.

Do not put your faith in religious tradition, superstition
or old wives tales. If it is not rooted in the Word of God,
do not believe it. There are many people who say, "I don't
know whether I believe in Jesus, but I believe in God."
That is not good enough. This faith power which God
shares with human beings is available only through Jesus
Christ.

It is not enough to say, "Jesus was a good man and I

follow His teachings." Without a relationship with Him, you will have no power to follow His teaching. The same power to create the good life is the power which allows you to live the good life. It is indwelling power put there by God, not something you make for your self. This power does not come from education or human connections. It is a gift given by God through Jesus Christ alone.

Perhaps you are facing a financial crisis right now and you picked this book hoping to find answers. True prosperity begins with Jesus. You will never be prosperous in the truest sense of the word until you accept Jesus Christ as your Lord and Savior. Do it now. Pray this prayer from your heart:

"Heavenly Father, I accept Jesus Christ as my Savior and Lord. I confess that He died on the cross for my sins, and was resurrected on the third day with all power in His hands. I receive the in-filling of the Holy Spirit and the spiritual gifts which He alone distributes. I repent of my sin, I renounce life without You. You are Lord of my life, with the Universe at Your command, and I am Your joint heir. Thank you Jesus."

If you prayed this prayer from the heart, you are born from above. You now have the faith of God and you qualify for everything He has.

2

2ND PRINCIPLE

"Pray It"

This commandment is a direct assault on the "religious" idea of prayer as ritual behavior intended to demonstrate one's piety. Once again you must ask yourself, "How badly do I want the destiny God has for me?" Do you want it badly enough to cast off traditions you have learned and to which you may be very attached. The purpose of prayer is to draw you into relationship with God, His love, His power and His plan for your life.

If you want prayer that brings results in life, you are going to have to discard the idea of prayer as a mere religious ritual. It must be real conversation with Reality Himself. Even "The Lord's Prayer" as a faithless recitation is a waste of time. If this offends you, your concern is in the wrong place. What is far more offensive is the empty, repetitive words people say because someone told them to, or they learned it from their family or Sunday School class. In fact Jesus warned against this kind of "prayer". "And when you pray, do not use vain repetitions as the heathen do. For they think they will be heard for their many words." (Matthew 6:7) On the other hand, something as familiar as The Lord's Prayer prayed with faith is powerful.

There are various kinds or expressions of prayer, which we will not delve into here. We are focusing on the prayer of petition and request. There is only one objective for praying this kind of prayer, and that is to get the results desired. This kind of prayer should be done with a spiritually violent determination to get what you are asking for.

Now I am going to give you a truth which shocks religious people, even some who are Christians. HUMAN BEINGS HAVE THE RIGHT TO MAKE DEMANDS ON GOD. God has given His creatures that right. While this may seem radical or disrespectful to you, I say it with all reverence for God. Once you give it a little thought, you will realize it makes perfect sense.

For example, every person who is saved makes a demand on God for their salvation. Christians do not come to God and say, "I accept Jesus Christ as my Lord and Savior. Now would you think about saving me? I don't want to go to hell and be separated from you for all eternity so think about saving me, please." Once you accept Jesus Christ as your Lord and Savior, God has no choice but to bring you into His family as a "born again" believer. When you take that step you make a demand on the transforming power of God, and something happens immediately.

In fact, the Greek word translated "ask" in the New Testament is aiteo, which means "to ask as of right." In other words it is not asking as in a "favor", but asking as in something "owed". You may be thinking, "On what basis does God owe me anything?" On the basis of the promises in His Word.

Know Who You Are

Many times we do not get results in prayer because we do not know how to pray. Some think that since God knows what we need before we ask it, how we pray makes no difference as long as we pray. Wrong! The scripture says "The effective, fervent prayer of a righteous man avails much." (James 5:16) The Greek word for "avails" is "ischuo" which means "has force, might, strength; works, makes whole". The word "much" is the Greek word "polus"(po.loos'), which means altogether abundant. Effective, fervent prayer has the force and might to bring results which are altogether abundant. This statement would be meaningless unless it carried with it the implied existence of the opposite, i.e., "ineffective" prayer. We can only contemplate effective prayer in light of the possibility of ineffective prayer.

The prayer which has force and brings powerful results has two qualities or characteristics. It is (1) effective - fervent and (2) made by the righteous. Who is the "righteous"? The answer is very simple. Those who are in Christ Jesus, who have accepted Him as Lord and Savior, are the "righteous." "For He [God] made Him [Jesus] who knew no sin to be sin for us, that we might become the righteousness of God in Him. (2Cor.5:21)

This will offend some Believers who have been taught the false piety that they are "just sinners saved by grace." This is a very wrong understanding of who Christians are in Christ. Nowhere in the Bible is that said or taught. Such sincere but false and misguided humility only hinders effective prayer. You cannot be a "sinner" and be "saved." Saved people do sin, but they are not "sinners."

A butterfly occasionally crawls, but it is not a caterpillar with wings. It is a butterfly. It was once a caterpillar, but it is no longer what it once was. If it were to think of itself as a caterpillar, it would continue to crawl. That is a perfect picture of where many Christians are in their spiritual lives - still crawling like caterpillars when they should be flying as butterflies.

Christ performed a great exchange in our behalf. Through the cross our sin became His sin, and His righteousness became our righteousness. When He cried out "My God, My God, why have You forsaken Me?"(Matthew 27:46), our sins had severed His fellowship with the Father. He had personally committed no sin, yet the Father had to turn away from His Son because our sins were placed upon Him.

The moment we accept Jesus Christ as our Lord and Savior, we become clothed in a new righteousness which is not our own, but Christ's. That righteousness is perfect, without a single blemish. When the scripture speaks then of "the righteous", it speaks of those who are in Christ Jesus.

Our prayer life is weakened when we base it on our own personal righteousness instead of the righteousness of Jesus Christ alone. When we feel we have slipped or failed, we think God does not and will not hear us. That is simply not so. The truth is that you are the third party beneficiary in a contract, which means the benefits to which you are entitled are the result of an agreement between two other parties. As a result, you can't affect those benefits because you are the beneficiary, not a controlling party. The Covenant which we benefit from is between God the Father and God the Son. It is sealed with the Son's blood. If it were sealed with our own blood, we would be controlling parties, but it is sealed with the precious blood of Jesus Christ.

For example, let us say that I entered into a contract to lend the money to build a factory. When the factory is built, the owner owes me millions. I then tell him I want the benefits paid to my children. He may think that arrangement is odd, but that money is mine to give to whomever I please.

The only responsibility of my children in the matter is to "receive" what I have provided for them. They start giving money to orphans, hospitals and the homeless, using their new wealth wisely and generously until one day they mistreat someone badly. Convicted by a sense of guilt, they begin to think to themselves, "We really don't deserve this money. We are not worthy. Each calls the factory owner and says, "Stop sending me those checks. I don't deserve it."

The owner says, "Sorry, I can't do that. My agreement is with your father. You are just the beneficiary. The terms were dictated by him. I have an agreement here which says you are to get this money. It's yours." You say, "You mean even though I messed up?" "That's right, and you may even mess up in the future, but that won't change my obligation to you because my agreement is with someone else in your behalf. Neither you nor I have authority to stop its benefits, and your father has promised he will never stop it."

That is the nature of God's Covenant. It is ultimately not with us, but for us through Jesus Christ. It was God's decision, and it is irreversible. All you need to do is accept what He has done for you. "If we confess our sins He is faithful and just to forgive us our sins and to cleanse us from all unrighteousness." (1John.1:9) The confession of the Believer must be, "I have been crucified with Christ; it is no longer I who live, but Christ lives in me; and the life which I now live in the flesh I live by the faith of the Son of God who loved me and gave Himself for me." (Galatians 2:20) You are the "righteous".

Do not be misled by traditional misunderstanding of scripture. We have all heard "There is none righteous, no not one." (Romans 3:9) That text is talking about unsaved mankind, not Believers. You must pray knowing that you have been made the righteousness of God through Jesus Christ. Only then will you come "boldly to the throne of grace, that you may obtain mercy and find grace to help in the time of need." (Hebrews 4:16)

If effective prayer has force and might to bring about wholly abundant results, then ineffective prayer is weak and brings little or no results. We want to avoid ineffective prayer at all costs. Effective prayer starts with the understanding that you have a right to make demands on God. That is not a right to disrespect God or to be irreverent in any way toward God. Nor does this mean that human beings have the right to "command" God or relate to God in any way other than awesome reverence.

The scripture says "ask and it shall be given". (Matthew7:7) The word "ask" is a translation of the Greek word "aiteo", which is defined by Strong's Exhaustive Concordance as "strictly a demand of something due." Making "demand" is used in the legal sense.

There are 8,000 promises in the Bible. Anytime you ask for something God has promised in His word, you are making demand for something due. It is not due because you have earned it or deserve it, but because God has promised it. He is obligated to grant your request. In fact He has obligated Himself to you.

No matter how you came to God, the relationship was initiated by Him. God says He owes you based on what Jesus Christ has done. At the highest price ever charged or paid, Christ bought your right to receive abundantly from God. As Elvina M. Hall's timeless song says, "Jesus paid it all, all to Him [we] owe. Sin had left a crimson stain, but He washed it white as snow."

Many people treat prayer as a kind of spiritual shopping in which you go into the store hoping to find the item you are looking for, but not knowing whether you can afford it. Actually prayer is more like going to the store to pick up what has already been picked out and paid for in advance. You go in to make demand that it be given you.

You ask politely; you even say "please." Nonetheless, the thought never crosses your mind that the answer would be "no". The cost has already been paid. The answer cannot be "no." "For all the promises of God in Him are Yes..." (2 Corinthians 1:20)

The Name of Jesus

When someone has made a promise and you ask them to follow through, the request is a bold demand for fulfillment. Every time you use the name of Jesus you invoke the promises of God. You pray in the name of Jesus not for the sake of tradition or ritual, but for authority and power; not because it sounds good, but because it works. Using His name means that your expectations are based on the blood bought Covenant of Jesus Christ, to which you are a legal heir.

The Covenant says He will heal you.(Psalm 107:20) The Covenant says He will prosper you.(Jeremiah 29:11) The Covenant says He will promote you.(Psalm 75:6,7) The Covenant says He will endow you with gifts and blessings from on high. (James 1:17) But you can only be brought into the Covenant through Jesus Christ. The name of Jesus carries the authority of the Covenant. We get the benefits, but He is the One who signed and sealed that contract with His own precious Blood.

When you pray in His name, you plead the Blood. When you pray in His name, you pray the Covenant. That is what we mean when we say there is power in the name of Jesus. There is healing in the name of Jesus. There is deliverance in the name of Jesus. There is salvation in the name of Jesus. You can get whatever you need in the name of Jesus. In fact the name "Jesus" is the anglo-ized version of the Hebrew name "Jehoshewah" or "Joshua" which means God is salvation, deliverance, health, victory and prosperity. The name of Jesus actually means prosperity in every way. Remember that every time you speak His name.

Knowing Where to Pray

We now know that in order for prayer to get results, it must be more than ritual or religious practice. It must come from the sincere heart, but it must also be based on right understanding. Those who have put our faith in Jesus Christ, who have been born again and filled with His Spirit, must approach God's throne boldly understanding that we are the righteousness of God in Christ Jesus.

God is merciful and kind, but He owes nothing to sinners other than salvation if they come through Jesus Christ. On the other hand, He must respond to those whom He has made His children and declared righteous. He has obligated Himself to those who are in Christ Jesus. Any other approach would dishonor the shed blood of His Only Begotten Son.

For prayer to get results we must not only know how to pray, but "where" to pray. Jesus once met a woman at a well who was very concerned about the place of worship. Her tradition said that Mount Gerizim was the place for Samarians to worship, but the Jews said that Jerusalem was the proper venue. Jesus made clear to her that God is not interested in whether she worshiped in Jacob's mountain or at Jerusalem. God is interested in being worshiped in spirit and in truth. Why then would I say it is important to know "where" to pray?

To answer this question we must go back to the text in which Jesus taught prayer. He said, "And when you pray..." (Matt.6:5) The word pray here is the Greek word, proseuchomai. It is a combination of two words, "pros"- which means toward or forward, and "*euchomai*", which means the will or desire. The word means literally "to will toward or for God". It implies much more than request. It suggests surrendering and aligning your will with God. Prayer then is an expression of oneness with God.

Prayer at its deepest level is lining up with God's will and plan for you. That is where the power of prayer lies. Elijah's prayers were powerful because they were an expression of the will of God. Jesus gave us insight into this when He said, "He who sent me is with me. The Father has not left me alone, for I do always those things that please Him". (John 8:29) We must abide in His word to be sure that our prayers are expressing His will. Then we know that our requests are pleasing to Him, and that they will be answered.

Jesus demonstrated this principle in the Garden of Gethsemane. He knew all too well that He was facing excruciating death by crucifixion. Death by crucifixion is one of the worst forms of torture human beings have ever devised. It is slow and excruciatingly painful. The muscles and tendons in the hands and feet are ripped as the weight of the body hangs from the cross. The lungs suffer slow paralysis. Every muscle feels the pain as they stretch and distort in response to the lack of oxygen . The person has to gasp for every breath. Seconds seem like days as the blood slowly drains from the body.

The spiritual suffering for Jesus had to be even worse than the physical pain. He suffered complete separation from the Father, spiritual death. For the first time in all eternity, His relationship with the Father would be broken. He would face the dark void of existence without God. He would become sin, and the Father would turn His back in rejection. That could only mean one destination - hell. Jesus knew what He was facing and prayed "O My Father, if it is possible, let this cup pass from me; nevertheless, not as I will, but as You will."

(Matt.26:39) He made this request, with the full commitment to submit to the will of the Father, wherever that led. So ought we to pray.

Jesus says when you pray don't be like the hypocrites who want to be seen by men. They want to impress people. But when you pray, go into your room or closet. The Greek word there means secret chamber or place of privacy. And when you have shut the entrance or the opening, pray to your Father Who is in secret. This text has usually been read at the surface level, but Jesus is saying something much deeper. He is saying, when you pray, go into that place where it is just you and God. That secret place to which no one has access but you and God. That's where your heavenly Father is. He is in that secret place in your heart, in your life. He is in the depths of your being. You rarely go there yourself.

Human beings tend to live superficial lives. We don't like to delve too deeply into our hearts because there are secrets we have tried to forget and scars we do not wish to see. God knows everything that is there and still loves you with a passion beyond human understanding. He has no desire to rub your face in the past. He wants to love and forgive you out of its bondage. He wants to meet you in the secret chamber of your soul, in the depth of your being. That is where He will change you forever. Are you willing to meet Him there?

The scripture says, "we do not know what to pray for as we ought" (Romans 8:26), but we have an insurance policy. "The Spirit Himself makes intercession for us with 'groaning' which cannot be uttered", unspeakable in human language. The Spirit speaks in our behalf from that secret place within us. That is why we are told to pray "in the spirit". When your spirit prays, the Holy Spirit can bring before God requests beyond what you can consciously ask or think. All effective prayer comes out of the depth of the human spirit. That is the "secret" place.

We get so caught up in facades and protecting our image. God does not crash the walls we build up. He desperately wants you to strip away the defenses and invite Him into the secret chamber of your soul, where you come face to face with the God who is Holy and Righteous altogether. He is there waiting for you. He already knows all the junk and baggage that is hidden and locked away. We have tried to forget it is there. God is ready to gently and lovingly clean house if you'll allow Him. "...[T]here is no creature hidden from His sight, but all things are naked and open to the eyes of Him to whom we must give account". (Heb.4:13)

Pray to your Father Who is in secret, and your Father who sees in secret will reward you openly. The Greek word for reward literally means He will "bring forth". That which you pray for in "secret" will be brought forth for all to see.

In one Biblical account the King of Assyria promised to destroy Jerusalem. He sent messengers to God's anointed, King Hezekiah, telling him and the people not to trust in the Lord. He also told the people not to listen to Hezekiah when he says trust God for deliverance. "No other gods have delivered any other people out of my hand," said the King of Assyria arrogantly. (2 Kgs.18:35)

The King of Israel turned to the most powerful weapon in his arsenal - prayer. "O Lord God of Israel,... You are God, You alone, of all the kingdoms of the earth. You have made heaven and earth. [S]ee... and hear the words of Sennacherib, which he has sent to reproach the living God. [N]ow therefore...save us from his hand, that all kingdoms of the earth may know that You are the Lord God, You alone." (2 Kings 19:15,19)

His prayer was answered. As Sennacherib was worshiping in the temple of his false god, his own sons struck him down with the sword. Hezekiah and his armies did not have to fight, not in the flesh. Every battle in life is a spiritual battle. They are fought and won not with men or money, but in the secret place of the spirit. The battle is not yours, but the Lord's. Stand still from striving and see through prayer the salvation of the Lord. Stand still in faith, and you will prevail.

Knowing What to Pray

Knowing "what" to pray is as important as knowing "where" to pray. Prayer should be the most uplifting experience a human being can have. Yet for many it is depressing and filled with fears and doubts. I remember having a deacon once who used to pray for me, "Lord, tear him down where he needs to be torn down." Thankfully God does not honor such prayers because there is no Christian commandment to pray for God to tear anybody down. Prayers like this come from religious tradition, not faith in Jesus Christ.

Often our prayers in behalf of ourselves are as negative. Some people may think their prayers are fervent and effective, but if they could listen to themselves, all they would hear is a rehearsal of everything that is wrong in their lives. They cry and moan to God about how bad things are. Where is the faith in such prayer? There is none. If you want to pray in a way that gets God's attention and power turned in your behalf, remember these very important principles:

Pray your vision, not your victimization. In other words, when you pray, do not talk to God only about the bad things you are experiencing in life. Talk to him about the life you want and hope to have. Make that the greatest part of your prayer.

Pray the solution, not the problem. If you are facing a particular problem, do not spend large amounts of time talking about how difficult the problem is. The more you talk about the problem, the bigger the problem becomes in your mind. The bigger you perceive the problem, the harder it is to operate in faith.

Pray your victory, not your defeat. If you ever get a life threatening diagnosis and prognosis from your doctor, do not start praying to make your peace with death.. Some people might start praying for the strength to die with dignity. They should be praying for overcoming power to defeat the challenge and emerge victorious. Pray, say and see yourself victorious over that disease, and you will experience miraculous results.

Do not accept the traditional, but very wrong notion that when it is your time, you'll go. Many people go before their time because of that attitude. Instead of fighting the good fight of faith and experiencing the victory that overcomes the world, they accept their "fate" and suffer defeat. The purpose of prayer is not to teach you to accept defeat, but to lead you into triumph. Jesus taught his disciples to pray, "Your kingdom come. Your will be done." (Matthew 6:10) He did not engage in a recitation of all the ways in which the will of God is not done, but simply that it be done, "[o]n earth as it is in heaven."

Is there anything evil or destructive in heaven? If Jesus prayed and taught us to pray that God's will be done on earth as it is in heaven, then the will of God for your life is for it to be like heaven on earth. The will of God for you is good in every way. Do not spend your time praying "acceptance" of anything that is not good, not from heaven. Your prayers will be lined up with God's will, and that's when they become powerful.

Five Keys to Powerful Prayer

1. Prayer must be positive. Pray your vision and your victory, not your victimization. Pray your solution, not your problem. Pray your hopes and dreams, never your fears and failures. Prayer will do you no good if it is filled with a recitation of all that is wrong in your life. Of course you should tell God your problems. He is your heavenly Father. Remember however that He knows what you need before you ask Him. (Matthew 6:8) You do not need to go on ad nauseam. He will help you. Therefore, spend the bulk of your time in prayer thanking and praising Him for the positive outcome you are seeking.

2. Prayer must be persuaded. If you are not absolutely persuaded that your prayers will be answered, you are wasting your time. The power of prayer is activated by faith that the thing desired will happen. People are sometimes frustrated that they do not get answers to prayer. That cannot be God's fault because He cannot lie or change. Nor do His promises change.

Therefore, when prayer goes unanswered, the fault must lie with us. Most of the time, it is in the area of being fully persuaded. That is why people are so quick to look for some answer beyond their own lack of faith. They can speedily find a reason to doubt that their petition will be fulfilled. James 1:6,7 says, "…ask in faith, with no doubting, for he who doubts is like a wave of the sea driven and tossed by the wind. For let not that man suppose that he will receive anything from the Lord…"

3. Prayer must be pointed. When it comes to your specific concerns, prayer does not work as a shot gun approach. It must be precise. For example, it is a waste of time to say, "Lord bless all the people in the world." In one sense, God already does that. He makes the sun shine and the rain fall on everyone. Of course, He does not bless everyone in the covenant sense in which He blessed Abraham and His seed.

Therefore, if you are in covenant relationship with God through Jesus Christ, it also makes no sense to pray, "Lord bless me." He already has. Or, "Lord be with me." He already is. What do you need? Be specific. Point your prayer toward your desire. Then you can actually measure the results.

4. Prayer must be persistent. Once you lock in on your desire, and you are sure that it is God's will for you, be tenacious about it. Be persistent. That does not mean that you continually ask God, but rather that you continually thank Him and praise Him for the answer. This is what Jesus taught; that people ought to pray and not lose heart. (Luke 18:1) He has already promised that you would have whatever you desire if you ask in faith. Therefore once you have asked in faith, do not continue begging God. He is your loving heavenly Father. He wants to meet your need. He has power to do so, but He puts the responsibility on you to bring about the result you desire through faith. Put to work the spiritual laws you have learned, and show yourself to be the child of your Father.

5. Prayer must be proclaimed. There is nothing wrong with silent prayer. I do it every day. Part of my prayer time however is spent talking to God in an audible voice which I can hear with my own ears. I use the power of the spoken word in my prayer life to reinforce my faith. When appropriate, you should confess your prayer requests to others, particularly those whom you are close to spiritually, and will agree with you in prayer. Jesus said that agreement in prayer among those in Covenant with Him enhances the power of their petition. (Matthew 18:10)

Remember that God is not pleased or moved by whining and crying about your troubles. God is moved and pleased by faith. If you want to move the heart of God, praise Him when things seem to be completely out of control. Praise Him when they seem to be beyond the point of no return. Praise Him when things look hopeless to anyone who does not trust God.

You will be amazed at how quickly and powerfully God will respond to your need. You are not praising Him because things have gone wrong. Your praise is an expression of trust that He will set them right, that all is well. You are praising Him in spite of any negative circumstances because your heart is steadfast trusting in the Lord. (Psalm 112:7)

Finally, while we have been discussing results in prayer, make sure that you do not forget that God is not a slot machine. He is Love. Love Him. Worship Him. Adore Him. Thank Him for being who He is and doing what He does. Do not reduce your relationship with God to meeting your needs. Base it on your desire to be in close fellowship with Him. "Draw near to God and He will draw near to you." (James 4:8) Which friend do you prefer - the one who only calls you only when in need or the one who keeps in touch all the time because she is interested in your life? The answer is obvious.

God wants relationship with you. He knows that you need His help, but since He has already committed to helping you, He wants to be more than that to you. God made Abraham a very wealthy man, but He made clear that the wealth was only a side benefit. "...Abram I am your shield, your exceedingly great reward." (Genesis 15:1) God wants you to have good health, a wonderful family, career and joyful life. Always keep in mind however, that the ultimate reward is God Himself. It does not get any better than having Him in your life.

3

3RD PRINCIPLE

"See It"

Proverbs 29:18 (KJV) says "where there is no vision the people perish." More modern translations say where there is no revelation or spiritual vision, the people cast off restraint, or engage in self-destruction. The issue is not whether you have vision, but whether you have God-inspired vision.

You have already learned that there is faith other than the faith of God. Just as there is false faith, there is also false vision. False vision leads to destruction. That is why the people perish when there is no God-given or God-inspired revelation or vision. That is why the wrong vision in the wrong hands is so very dangerous.

Just before God brought judgment through the flood, He saw the wickedness of man was great in the earth. Notice what God calls attention to after pointing out the great wickedness of man: "…and that every imagination of the thoughts of his heart was only evil continually." (Gen.6:5,6)

God does not give a laundry list of the evils, but rather points to the underlying reality, the wickedness of mankind's vision. The word translated "imagination" is the Hebrew word "*yatzer*" which means to imagine, envision or frame in the mind. It is the creation of a picture or blueprint in the mind and heart.

The Hebrew word for "build" is a derivative, "*yatzar*". The two words are almost identical. God is teaching us this principle: "To envision [or imagine] is to create." The creative power of the vision within is released when that vision is spoken and acted upon. It must first be in you as an inner image. When God said, "Let there be light," He already imagined it before He spoke it. It was already in Him before it came out of Him in a visible manifestation.

Jesus said, "[O]ut of the abundance of the heart the mouth speaks. A good man out of the good treasure of his heart brings forth good things, and an evil man out of the evil treasure [of his heart] brings forth evil things." (Matt.12:34,35) To imagine in the heart and speak from the mouth is to bring forth or create.

The vision which creates (1) comes from the heart, and (2) is a matter of continuous preoccupation, meditation and action until the vision is realized. The reason why man was wicked was that his vision had become wicked. When Satan was tempting Eve, his goal was to give her a vision for herself contrary to the will of God. Once he accomplished that, it was very easy to get her to behave wickedly. After her discussion with the serpent, the very tree which had been in the garden all along looked different. Her vision was altered, and she then "...saw that the tree was good for food, that it was pleasant to the eyes and a tree desirable to make one wise…" (Genesis 3:6)

In the story of the tower of Babel (Gen.11:1-9), the problem is not human ability, but the wickedness of the human heart. "Let us build ourselves a city;…make a name for ourselves." They have a vision, but it does not include God. God Himself admits that because of the unity of their vision "nothing they propose to do will be withheld from them."

God had to intervene to limit their power and overthrow their wicked devices. Their unified vision made their destructive power virtually unlimited. If this seems far-fetched, consider what happened when Germany unified around the vision of Adolph Hitler. Only an equally unified vision for good could overcome it. A vision of good inevitably overcomes a vision of evil. The problem is "where there is no vision [of good] the people perish." (Proverbs 29:18) There is more than one kind of vision. There is wicked vision. The word "wicked" means "twisted" as in a wicker basket or the wick of an oil lamp. To envision that which is contrary to the will of God is to be morally and spiritually twisted.

Abortion, sexual immorality, political corruption, fraud, theft and every societal evil come out of man's fallen nature which results in twisted vision. In the tower of Babel incident, the people's vision was unrestrained by submission to God. Indeed their vision was a direct challenge to God. Wicked vision carries the mark of Satan. Hitler, Stalin and other bloodthirsty despots have proved that. Of course human beings, following their selfish desires have plenty of capacity for wickedness without an evil charismatic leader to help them.

There is also "Human vision". God gives us human vision to meet our daily needs. Once I had to move a very large, heavy desk into my home. It had to be carried up a flight of stairs and through a narrow doorway. I saw in my mind how to move that desk. When the movers brought it to the house, I followed exactly the plan that I saw. That was human vision, not divine revelation.

People use human vision to make money, to invent new products, to create art and buildings, etc. This is of course God-given ability which humans have. It is why we invented automobiles, bridges, skyscrapers, toasters and today's technological revolution. This ability and what it produces can be turned to good or evil.

Then there is Divine vision or revelation. God wants to inspire the human spirit with what comes directly out of His own heart. This book is a vision born out of my relationship with God. It comes out of His heart of love for people and desire to empower us with the spiritual wisdom needed to transform our lives. God wants to impart a vision to stretch and expand your thinking. Perhaps you have been mulling over an idea, seeing something in your heart which could contribute to the betterment of your life and others. Only by embracing and pursuing it can you tap into its power to change your life and the lives of others.

Without vision, life shrinks instead of expanding. It becomes smaller and more confining. A powerful, inspiring vision infuses your life with energy and purpose. Where there is vision, the people prosper. Vision expands your capacity. It will not allow you to accept the present limitations. You will throw them off. This is what Divine vision does, and why it is essential for living a successful life. That is why the scripture says without it, "the people perish."

As your vision is, so will your life be. Or to put it differently, "Your vision determines your destiny." Consider the story of Lot's escape from Sodom and Gomorrah. (Genesis 19) The angels say to Lot, "Escape for your life! Do not look behind you, nor stay anywhere in the plain. Escape to the mountains, lest you be destroyed." Lot's family had become infected with the spirit of Sodom and Gomorrah. They benefited from it even if they did not directly participate in the wickedness themselves.

They were to be delivered, but God told them not to look back.

He was telling them to turn their eyes away from the wickedness of Sodom and Gomorrah. It was time to see a different future. Lot's wife could not resist the temptation to look at the limitations of the past rather than the vast expanse of the future. She looked back and became a pillar of salt. Her vision determined her destiny.

The life of Job is usually seen as a lesson in the value of suffering. A careful study of Job teaches another lesson. Job was an upright man who feared God, and shunned evil. He was also the wealthiest man in the East. The devil proposes that God touch "all that he [Job] has...he will surely curse You to your face." (Job 1:11).

Notice first that contrary to popular understanding, Satan does not propose that he himself should harm Job, but that God should do it. Pay close attention to God's answer: "Behold, all that he has is in your power." (Job 1:12) The word "behold," simply means "Look." God was saying Job was already in Satan's power. Why was this so?

Although Job was very successful, he was also a man of extreme anxiety. He had a vision within himself that was working against the good life he had experienced. Job's wife gets bad press for saying to Job, "Do you still hold fast to your integrity? Curse God and die." (Job 2:9) Why did she say that? Her husband was actually the person preoccupied with cursing God, and he very likely sowed that seed into his wife. "...[He would rise early in the morning and offer burnt offerings...For Job said, 'It may be that my sons have sinned and cursed God in their hearts.' (Job 1:5) The first person to talk about cursing God wasn't Job's wife. It wasn't even Satan. It was Job himself. Satan knew that this was an area of major worry and concern for Job. That's why he made the accusation to God.

Job was a man filled with fear. He tells us himself, "The thing that I greatly feared has come upon me, And what I dreaded has happened to me." (Job 3:25) Worry is negative vision, based on fear. Hope is God-inspired vision based on faith. Fear activates and empowers Satan in our lives the same way faith activates and empowers God in our lives.

Fear is twisted or wicked faith. It is faith in death and destruction. It is belief in the worst. Although it may not be our conscious intent, for a Believer to live in fear, doubt and worry is to call God a liar. It is to say, "I do not trust You with my future." That is the same as saying you do not trust God's love, power or desire to do you good. Let me reassure you. God can be trusted. I have 40 years of experience to prove it.

The miracle of Jesus walking on water is a lesson on the power of vision. Peter saw Jesus perform this feat and said, "Lord... command me to come to You on the water." Jesus said, "Come." Peter is the second person in human history to walk on water, but something went wrong. "When he saw that the wind was boisterous, he was afraid; and beginning to sink..." (Matthew 14:28-30) Remember however that wind cannot be seen, only its effects. Peter caught the right "vision" when he "saw" Jesus walking on the water. He caught the wrong "vision" when he "saw" the wind. Once his vision changed to one of sinking because of the force of the wind, his destiny changed and he began to sink. At first, Peter was walking into Biblical history. A moment later, a vision of failure took hold, and he was headed for the bottom of the sea.

Like Lot's wife, many Christians are looking in the wrong direction, at the wrong things. The experiences of Job and Peter teach us what happens when our minds are filled with fear and dread. We are drawn toward death and destruction. When our hearts are filled with faith and hope in God, we are drawn toward life, to fulfill our destiny.

What Do You See?

What do you want out of life? If you want little, you will see little. If you "see" little, you will have little. On the other hand, you can want much, but "see " little and still end up with little. The key is not just in wanting, but in "seeing" or envisioning. Most people want something better out of life than what they have. They sometimes try various methods of "getting", but find themselves frustrated. They work harder for longer hours only to find that the government is the chief beneficiary. They get deeper in debt, more fatigued and unable to ever enjoy the fruits of their labor. Think of the millions who have slowly perished, striving without the results they desire. That may describe your life or the life of someone you know.

"Where there is no vision the people perish." Where there is vision, people prosper. Have you ever considered that nothing created in the material world was created without there first being a vision, a blueprint for what that "thing" would be?

Even you and I are the result of a vision in the heart and mind of God. "...God said, 'Let us make man in Our image, according to our likeness...'" (Genesis 1:26) God said in effect, "I'm going to make man based on the image I have of what a physical creature would look and act like if it were made to have My attributes, i.e., be in My likeness." In fact God even wrote down that image (Psalm 139:16), which is another principle we will cover later.

Even a person who does not believe in God must admit that all humanly created objects begin with a vision in the mind or heart of a human being. That is also where the life you desire begins. Do you want to be wealthy, but see no way for it to happen? Determine never to think again, "I don't see a way."

Start to see yourself out of debt with abundant finances to help yourself and others.

Are you having marital difficulties? More important than counseling, discussion and other approaches to healing a damaged relationship is the vision you have of where that relationship is going. If you have already convinced yourself that your marriage will not improve, it won't. If what you see in your future is divorce, you'll have it. Your vision predicts your future.

This should not be difficult to accept. Medical doctors have now discovered that even a patient who is deathly ill can have a miraculous impact on her condition by envisioning the future in a state of health. There have been experiments in the use of positive visioning in promoting wellness. A patient is told to "see" white cells attacking and destroying infectious cells, and the body responds by carrying out the blueprint the mind is conveying to it.

Why does this work? It works because it is the way God designed this physical universe to work. The greatest force in the universe is not atomic energy; it is spiritual energy. The energy which created the universe and all physical matter is the power of God. That power is infinitely creative. The New Testament calls it "dunamis" in the Greek. Our English transliteration is "dynamite". Dunamis is explosive power without being destructive. Its ability to shape circumstances is as intricate or expansive as is needed to achieve any objective.

Since God is love, the vision you have should be based upon the love of the One Who created you to love and be loved. His vision for you is only good. When God looked at all He made, His conclusion was that it was very good. The crowning glory of His creation is mankind, created to be like Him. Your vision must be based upon love for oneself and others. That will inform your vision in a far more effective way than relying on your own prejudices, pre-dispositions and feelings of inadequacy and unworthiness.

We learn from the Bible that those who put their faith in Jesus Christ, are declared worthy by God. "For He made Him who knew no sin to be sin for us, that we might become the righteousness of God in Him." (2 Corinthians 5:21) You are worthy to have every good thing life has to offer. You have to see it that way before you will ever have it that way.

How Focused Are You?

The realization of your vision will not happen through an occasional passing thought. The use of vision requires focus. Jesus said, "The lamp of the body is the eye. If therefore your eye is good, your whole body will be full of light. But if your eye is bad, your whole body will be full of darkness. If therefore the light that is in you is darkness, how great is that darkness!" (Matthew 6:22,23) Jesus is not talking here about physical sight, but spiritual sight or vision. The Old King James Version uses the word "single" instead of "good." If you are not focused on seeing things God's way and only God's way, you are in darkness. If you see yourself a sinner, sick, poor, weak, held down, kept back, and in trouble, you are in darkness. And "how great is that darkness."

There is no darkness in God. If you are saved, you are not a sinner; the word says you are the very righteousness of God. If you are sick, He sees you healed and healthy. If you are poor, He sees you rich. If you are weak, He sees you strong. God's Word says, "Let the weak say I am strong." (Joel 3:10) If you are held down, kept back and in trouble, He sees you coming up and breaking out of every bondage. He wants to deliver you and honor you. Your task is to get your vision in complete agreement with God's vision for your life. Anything else comes from the enemy, Satan. He means to see you fail in every way just as much as God intends for you to succeed in every way. The text also deals with focus. The "good" eye is a translation of a Greek word which means "clear and focused". You must see your vision with focused clarity and detail.

As you travel toward your destiny, you must be attentive to the signs and landmarks which indicate you are on the right road. Traveling a familiar road requires little concentration, but when you set out on a road you've never traveled to a new destination, you must focus to be sure you do not miss turns and forks along the way.

You must focus on your destination with considerable intensity. I strongly recommend setting aside time each day to pray and meditate. In fact, doing it several times a day is even better. You will make more progress in life with this spiritual discipline than you will ever achieve worrying, wondering and working longer hours. "Let your eyes look straight ahead, And your eyelids look right before you. Ponder the path of your feet, And let all your ways be established."(Proverbs 4:26)

What Are You Focused On?

"Turn away my eyes from looking at worthless things, And revive me in your way." (Psalm 119:37)

If the concept of vision seems unfamiliar, be assured that it is already at work in your life. The question is whether it has been working for you or against you. Every time worry and fear make you see the worst outcome, you are using vision. If you spend your time watching TV and movies filled with immoral violence and illicit sex, you are filling your mind with those images. Many youth are committing acts of violence and sexual promiscuity like their heroes on television, in movies and on the street. They feed on a steady diet of "thug life." They preoccupy themselves with the vile and profane.

We should not be surprised that they think, talk and act like the images they see and often become what those images represent. Alcoholics and drug addicts are often children who grew up with that image of adulthood portrayed by their parents and others. They could not wait to experience intoxication as they have seen Mom or Dad do so often. They fulfilled the 'vision" instilled in them, to their destruction. I started smoking as a teenager to look like my father and others I saw smoking. They looked so cool to me. I actually had to work at becoming addicted to nicotine. When I first started, smoking made me nauseous. I persisted until I could smoke with the best of them.

Thankfully, a different vision took root in me several years later and I quit, never to smoke another cigarette. The new vision of myself as a non-smoker changed my lifestyle and ultimately changed my destiny.

Stay With It

"Therefore I have set my face like a flint, and I know that I will not be ashamed." (Isaiah 50:7)

This is not easy. It requires focus and discipline and intentionality. It is certainly easier than beating your head against the brick wall of frustration. It is easier than sleepless nights, high blood pressure, heart attack and stroke. It is easier than pushing yourself into an early grave. However, you must practice patience. Scripture admonishes, "For you have need of endurance (patience), so that after you have done the will of God, you may receive the promise." (Hebrews 10:36) Another verse says, "[L]et patience have its perfect work, that you may be perfect and complete, lacking nothing." (James 1:4)

You want to succeed in every area of life. You want a prosperous marriage. You want a prosperous career or business. You want to prosper mentally, socially, physically and financially. You must be fully committed to master anything that is important to you. You must have your "face like a flint". That phrase comes from a Messianic text in the Hebrew Scriptures which speaks of the suffering of Jesus. He knew that His glory was to be realized by way of the cross. Jesus was undeterred, committed to fulfilling His destiny as Savior of the world. You do not have nearly the hurdle to overcome or the destiny to achieve that Jesus did. Yet you can access and implement the same spiritual power He used.

You are going to have to turn off the television, discard some of your wasteful activities and spend more time in prayer, meditation and fellowship with God. You are going to have to be as competent in these things as you have been in worry, anxiety and avoidance.

When your vision of the best that life has to offer becomes more real within you than the circumstances around you, success will overtake you. When your vision becomes the very air you breathe, you will create prosperity. Set your vision on spiritual, emotional, mental, physical, and financial well-being, and you will have it.

4

4TH PRINCIPLE

"Speak It"

Y ou are made in the image of God. You have been given the attributes of God. He is the Supreme Being - Omniscient, Omnipotent and Omnipresent. He knows all, sees all, hears all, is everywhere at the same time and has no limit to His power. He is the Almighty.

But as children of God, we are like our Heavenly Father. All that God does, you and I do, with limitations of course. We have His Divine attributes in finite measure. Jesus said in John 3 that you can "see" the kingdom of God and "enter" the Kingdom of God by being born again, born from above. The "Kingdom" is not some empty religious concept. In the Greek, the word translated "Kingdom" means "reign" or "realm."

The Kingdom of God is simply God's way of doing things or the spiritual system or realm in which God operates. He allows His children to enter and operate in that realm. It is the realm where the Spirit of God and the angels of God operate. It is not chaotic, unpredictable and frightening. God's realm is more orderly, more real and far more powerful than the physical realm in which we humans usually function.

Some people put their faith in good luck charms, fortune tellers, tea leaf and taro card readers, horoscopes, witchcraft or even communicating with the dead. This is how they relate to and contact the supernatural world. All these things are an are an attempt to counterfeit the legitimate and awesome power that is available to us through Almighty God. The counterfeits invoke the destructive power of Satan and demonic forces. If you are a Christian, there should be no need to warn you about these things. You should already know better. If you are not a Christian, and you have been exploring the exercise of spiritual power through something other than the Word of God, these things can only do you harm in the end.

There is a consequence to spending counterfeit money because it is not real. Therefore anything you buy with it is not legitimately yours. You will be caught and punished. Trying to conjure up illegitimate spiritual forces is similar. You are deceived to think anything you gain from it is real. You are also enslaving yourself to forces that mean you no good.

The key to the very best in life is God. You do not have a financial, marital or job problem; you have a spiritual problem. Every problem should be attacked first be through spiritual principles - the power of prayer, faith and the Word of God.

Speak the Word

Jesus said, "It is the Spirit who gives life; the flesh profits nothing. The words that I speak to you are spirit and they are life." (John 6:63) Notice something very important. God was unwilling to leave His Word in the realm of silence. He speaks, and His words are full of power. That power creates and enhances life.

The first chapter of Genesis reveals God's creative power. It gives a bleak description of earth's condition: "The earth was without form and void and darkness was upon the face of the deep. And the Spirit of God was hovering over the face of the waters. (Genesis 1:2) When one looks to the original language, the word for "without form" is the Hebrew word "*tohuw*" which means that the earth was "waste, desolate, empty and worthless".

The word "void" is a similar Hebrew word, "*bohuw*", which refers to an empty, indistinguishable ruin. The "darkness" mentioned in the text is not merely physical darkness. We know this condition is not authored by God. For "...God is light and in Him is no darkness at all." (1 John 1:5) The

The Hebrew word for darkness, "*choshek*", means misery, destruction, death, ignorance, sorrow and wickedness. Verse two of the first chapter of Genesis paints a picture which seems hopeless. Three words are the prelude to light and creativity: "Then God said," God's response to the darkness was to speak. He called light into being with the power of His word.

Read Genesis, Chapter one and notice that verses 3, 6, 9, 11, 14, 20, 24 all include the same powerful phrase, "And God said." The creative power of God was exercised through the spoken word, even in the creation of man. Verse 26 says, "Then God said, Let Us make man in Our image, according to our likeness..."

Mankind was made by God to be like God. Only God, man and angels use words. All other creatures are bound by their instinct. They cannot decide by acts of will to behave contrary to that instinct. A dog who saves his master's life is using instinct and training. There may well be a spiritual dimension to the relationship between him and the owner, but only the owner has made a conscious decision to love and care for his pet. The dog has no such capacity. He is created with inherent ability to respond to his owner's love, but not to will or to decide intellectually. Human beings make spiritual and intellectual decisions as do no other creatures on earth. That ability is closely related to the gift of language with which we reason and decide.

Words are not merely an expression of who we are, but the means whereby we create and shape who we are and the environment around us. Through this power we can change our circumstances in the same way that God rid Himself of the darkness and desolation facing Him. Likewise, the words you use articulate the vision within your heart and ultimately determine your destiny.

God's First Commandment to Man

After God created the crown jewel of His universe, man and woman, He "blessed" them. This should not be treated lightly.

The "blessing" of God is an empowerment. It is authority accompanied by power. Then God gave a commandment as to what should be done with this authority and power. "...God said to them, Be fruitful and multiply, fill the earth and subdue it, have dominion..." (Genesis 1:28)

The first part of God's command to His God-like creature is to be creative. That is what it means to be fruitful and multiply. This is not limited to having children. It speaks to the whole range of human endeavor. Then God says, "Have dominion." He says in effect, "You are to be My under-rulers, kings and queens over the earth. How does a king rule? A King rules by the authority of his word. Governments are run by the authority of words. You can rule over the circumstances of your life by the authority of your words. God never intended for human beings to be victims of circumstance. He intended for us to rule over circumstances.

This is the exalted status God gave to man. Psalm 82:6 says, "I said, 'You are gods, and all of you are children of the Most High.'" Jesus reaffirms this statement during a debate over His right to call Himself the Son of God. "Is it not written in your law, 'I said, "You are gods"? ...He called them gods, to whom the word of God came (and the scripture cannot be broken)..." (John 10:34,35) The scripture speaks for itself. All we need do is accept it with humility.

The Tools of Supernatural Authority

From a biblical perspective, words are the very stuff of the universe. "In the beginning was the Word, and the Word was with God, and the Word was God...All things were made through Him, and without Him nothing was made that was made." (John 1:1,3) We have already learned how God created by calling or speaking "things" into being. Even scientists admit that DNA is a kind of language, a blue print for the design of each living thing.

The unseen power - the spiritual DNA - behind all that is visible and invisible is God's Word. The same power which created is the power which sustains. "In Him was life, and the life was the light of men." (John 1:4) When things are boiled down to the point beyond which science can reach, there is God. Our lives did not emerge from the prehistoric ooze as a cosmic accident. We are the very intentional creation of Him whose Word is absolute power.

Not only were all things created by His Word, but all creation is set in order by that same Word. "By faith we understand that the worlds were framed by the Word of God..." (Hebrews 11:3) That word "framed" is a translation of a Greek word which means that the cosmos was completely and thoroughly set in order by the Word of God. That order is then sustained by His Word. "…[I]n Him all things consist." (Colossians 1:17) His Word holds all things together.

This should not be difficult for Americans to understand. Our country more than any nation in history, is held together by "words". Former President John Adams said, "We are a nation of laws and not of men." Laws are words by which citizens of a free nation agree to be governed. Because of that agreement those words hold us together and sustain the order and prosperity of our country.

To the extent those laws are rooted in eternal truth, they cannot be overturned. Sadly, more and more Americans are rejecting the truth of God's word and making up a morality which suits them. The problem is that laws rooted in man's selfish desires cannot be sustained. People are free to do this, but their actions will never be legitimate. Man is incapable of manufacturing divine approval or the inner satisfaction which goes with it.

That is why many on the left of the political spectrum engage in the very bullying they decry. They are angry and mean spirited because their lives are lived in rebellion against God. This can be true of anyone regardless of political persuasion. They engage in the very bullying they decry. The inner peace and satisfaction they need eludes them because their lives are out of sync with Gods design.

Their real argument is with the Bible and the enemy

...ney seek to destroy is God. The problem is that neither God nor His Word can be defeated. My prayer is that they will repent and accept God's word before it is too late. There is no justifying sin, no matter how natural that sin may feel. God's Word is law, and nothing can resist it. It will break whatever and whomever tries to overcome it.

Nothing in the natural world, animate or inanimate, can cause God's Word to cease operation or become void of power. His Word holds the universe together. Likewise your words hold your personal universe together. The things you say either create or destroy. "You will declare a thing, And it will be established for you." (Job 22:28)

Your universe is your sphere of influence, the circumstances which surround your life, over which you have been given authority. We will take up the issue of authority in detail later, but suffice to say right now that your word carries authority in your "realm." God made it that way. You wield that authority by your words the same way God wields authority by His words. We all know this to be true, but most of us have not thought about it. A man or woman arrives home from work. The words that are spoken when he or she walks through the door can set the atmosphere for the entire evening, good or bad. In one sentence, you can create anger and tension, or peace and joy.

You may read this and say to your self, "That is ridiculous. I can't change anything by talking." Is that so? Scientific studies have shown that the destiny and behavior of a child can be dramatically altered by the words spoken to that child. If the words spoken are words of failure, discouragement and worthlessness, that child's behavior will mirror those words.

Life responds to words. How many wives are depressed and discouraged with their husbands and marriages because of the words that husband speaks to his wife? Do you remember when people expressed amazement to learn that even plants respond to the human voice, that speaking to plants causes them to become healthier. Jesus taught this lesson 2,000 years ago when He spoke to a fruitless fig tree and caused it to wither within 24 hours.

Jesus taught the importance of the spoken word and commended those who understood this. One of the greatest commendations He gave was to a man who expressed the faith that all Jesus needed to do was speak the Word: "...[A] centurion came to Him, pleading with Him, saying, 'Lord my servant is lying at home paralyzed, dreadfully tormented' And Jesus said to him, 'I will come and heal him.' The centurion answered and said, 'Lord, I am not worthy that you should come under my roof. But only speak a word, and my servant will be healed...' When Jesus heard it, He marveled, and said to those who followed, 'Assuredly, I say to you, I have not found such great faith, not even in Israel!'" (Matthew 8:5-8,10)

Jesus demonstrated the power of words when He spoke to that fig tree:

"Now in the morning, as He returned to the city, He was hungry. And seeing a fig tree by the road, He came to it and found nothing on it but leaves, and said to it, "Let no fruit grow on you ever again." Immediately the fig tree withered away. And when the disciples saw it, they marveled. Jesus reassured them, "?..I say to you, if you have faith and do not doubt, you will not only do what was done to the fig tree, but also if you say to this mountain 'Be removed and be cast into the sea,' it will be done." (Matthew 21:18-21)

The lesson is not how to kill a plant, but how to rid yourself of something that is a hindrance in your life. Obstacles to our progress need to be removed. You may have a bad habit that is holding you back. It could be something as seemingly benign as watching too much television which is robbing you of productive time. It could be a relationship which has you emotionally entangled, and is blocking you from a better life. It could be a physical malady or illness which has plagued you. Jesus did not play around with an unfruitful "thing". He used the authority of His Word to remove it.

This was a lesson to His disciples about the power of their words, spoken in faith. When they asked Him how He did this, He said to them, in effect, "A fig tree is nothing. You can even move mountains if you believe and speak just as you have seen Me do." Sometimes there are mountains in our lives, but you will never move the mountains if you do not know how to speak to fig trees. You will not bring supernatural power to bear on the big things if you do not first learn to use it in smaller matters.

The Driving Force

Not only is the spoken word the power which sets and keeps all things in order. It is also the force which keeps all things moving. It is the unseen energy source behind the very rotation of electrons around the nucleus of an atom. Scientists tell us that there are 6 trillion actions taking place in the human body at any given moment. That is a staggering amount of activity.

Consider the movement going on at the atomic level in every piece of matter which exists on the earth, in the sea, in this solar system, this galaxy, the universe. It is mind boggling. Yet it is all happening in order, according to a prearranged system designed by the Supreme Designer. Mega-trillions of activities on the macro and micro levels all occurring at once, sustained by an unseen energy in the universe which never runs out.

That unseen force driving the universe is the Word of God. "God...has in these last days spoken to us by His Son, through Whom also He made the worlds; who being the brightness of His glory and the express image of His person, and upholding all things by the word of His power..." (Hebrews 1:1-3) The word "upholding" is the translation of the Greek word "enegko" which means carrying, bearing, driving – as in the force behind something moving. The force you need to drive your circumstances in a different direction is not anger, aggression or more hours spent on the job. The true force is the word power you have been given by God to "carry" you where you are supposed to go.

How Does it Work?

The Word of God has been made available to humanity, placed in a book for our access. We can read it, study it and meditate it. The power of that Word is now in the hands of human beings. Our own needs and desires must yield to the will of God. This is God's intention. John 1:12 says, "As many as received Him, to them He gave the right to become children of God, to those who believe in His name." The word "right" in the text is a translation of the Greek word "exousia". It actually means "authority", "jurisdictional power", "liberty", "superhuman mastery", "delegated influence".

God has given His authority, His jurisdiction, to His children. You have been given the authority to function as a child of God, using the Word of God. When a judge has "jurisdiction", his word is law. This is one of the reasons why many Christians needlessly fail. Tradition has taught them to pray and leave the rest in the hands of God. Scripture says however that each believer has been given a sword, which is clearly an offensive weapon. That sword is the Word of God. A sword is a meaningless weapon unless it is wielded. God does not wield the sword for us. He placed it in our hands.

This is part of the spiritual weaponry we must use to gain victory over Satan. God expects His people to use every tool - every weapon - at our disposal.

God said to Joshua, the great leader who succeeded Moses, "This Book of the Law shall not depart from your mouth..." (Joshua 1:8) In other words, "You are to speak in agreement with the words in this book all the time." He wanted Joshua to be sure that the spiritual power of his words worked for him, not against him. The way to do that is to line our words up with the Word of God. In this way, we line ourselves up with His power, His will and His plan for our lives.

God's Words must become your words. How does this happen? God tells Joshua, "...[Y]ou shall meditate in it day and night..." We will cover this subject in much greater detail later, but it is important to understand that nothing will come out of your heart that is not put there. People curse and utter vile things because those things are in their hearts. They were put there in most cases by what people hear, see and say. Spouses, parents, friends, colleagues, popular culture can speak terrible things into people's lives. Children are particularly vulnerable.

What comes out of the mouth is what is in the heart, and those words will either enrich or poison you and those around you. Jesus said, "For out of the abundance of the heart the mouth speaks. A good man out of the good treasure of his heart brings forth good things, and an evil man out of the evil treasure brings forth evil things." (Matthew 12:34)

Here is a paradox. What you speak comes from the heart, and what you speak goes into your heart. Therefore you must guard your heart by refusing to allow any unworthy thought to proceed from your mouth. It may run through your mind, but it does not have to go into your heart. Someone once said, "You cannot stop birds from flying over your head, but you can stop them from nesting in your hair." The moment you speak that negative thought, you have given it direct access to the core of your being, "But those things which proceed out of the mouth come from the heart, and they defile a man." (Matthew 15:18)

Therefore the way you keep your heart clean is to put the right things in and keep the wrong things out. Do not meditate on or speak what is evil. "[W]hatever things are true, whatever things are noble, whatever things are just, whatever things are pure, whatever things are lovely, whatever things are of good report, if there is any virtue and if there is anything praiseworthy - meditate on these things." (Philippians 4:8)

The instruction God gave Joshua allowed him to experience astounding success. We still sing, "Joshua fought the battle of Jericho and the walls came tumbling down." Joshua caused the sun to stand still in its place while he defeated his enemies. There are those who say that is a myth, but why would the God who made the sun not be able to make it stand still if He chooses? It is astounding that God would use a human being to accomplish such a remarkable feat, but He also wants to accomplish miracles through you.

The same formula which guided Joshua into the realm of supernatural success will also guide you. God says to us what He said to Joshua. If you keep my word in your mouth, and "you meditate in it day and night... you may observe to do according to all that is written in it." In other words, you will "see" how to get things done. "For then you will make your way prosperous and have good success." God did not promise to make Joshua's way successful. He promised that Joshua would be empowered to do it himself. God shows us "the path of life," but we must walk it out.

This is where many sincere believers are misguided. Some Christians have been taught the traditional but very wrong idea that God makes people sick and impoverished to teach them humility, There is a trap at the other extreme of thinking that God automatically heals or prospers whomever He chooses. This is also wrong. Deuteronomy 8:18 says, "And you shall remember the Lord your God, for it is He who gives you power to get wealth, that He may establish His covenant which He swore to your fathers, as it is this day." It does not say that God gives you wealth. It says that God gives you power to get it. There is a major difference. The Word of God tells you how to get it. You can love God with all your heart, and remain poor unless you put to work the principles that bring wealth. Success is not automatic.

Word Confessions

Part of the new motivational teaching by success coaches these days is positive affirmations. They can be as bizarre as Shirley McClain affirming in the mirror, "I am God." Or they can be as benign as Tony Robbins having you confess overwhelming success in your life. Some, like McClain's can be extremely destructive because they dishonor the only true and living God.

Positive affirmations can be helpful, because all words can influence. The problem is that words completely disconnected from the True Source of prosperity are potentially dangerous.

"For what profit is it to a man if he gains the whole world, and loses his own soul?" (Matthew 16:26) Words can be used to bless or to curse. Witchcraft uses words to try to gain power over people. Liars use words to deceive people. They will reap what they sow.

The words that have power to transform your life for good must be rooted in truth. The Word of God is truth. What should you confess? That depends upon what your need is at a given moment. The range of possibilities is too large to exhaust here, but a few examples will be helpful.

If you are facing financial difficulty, you might confess: "wealth and riches will be in [my] house." Psalm 112:3; "God has pleasure in my prosperity." Psalm 35:27; "The blessing of the Lord makes [me] rich and He adds no sorrow to it." Proverbs 10:22; "I shall be a joy, a praise and an honor before all who hear all the good that God does to me; they shall fear and tremble for all the goodness and all the prosperity that God provides for me." Jeremiah 33:9; "The wealth of the sinner is laid up for me." Proverbs 13:22; "God has given me riches and wealth, and given me power to eat of it, to receive my

heritage and rejoice in my labor – this is the gift of God."
Ecclesiastes 5:19.

I have paraphrased and personalized these texts to
help you use them in your own life. You may wonder what
gives anyone the right to use scripture this way? God has
given us His word. It belongs to those who have accepted
Jesus Christ as Lord and Savior. When you do that, you
become heir to every promise in Scripture. If you've
never done that, pray this simple prayer, from your heart:

*"Heavenly Father, I want to live for you, to serve you
and to experience the best life possible here on earth. I
also want to be with you for all of eternity. I know that the
only way these things become possible is through Jesus
Christ. I now accept Him as my Lord and Savior. I believe
that He died on the cross for my sins, was buried, went into
hell and was resurrected on the third day with all power
in His hands. I know that as a result of this confession, I
am born again, saved and enter into the Kingdom of God.
When I die, I will come to heaven and be with you for all
of eternity. All of the promises of the New Covenant are
now mine. I am your child, and I thank you for receiving
me. In Jesus Name, Amen."*

If you just prayed this prayer from your heart, you
are now a born again child of God. You now need to find
a Word based church to teach you how to experience
victory. From this point on, you no longer need ask, "What
gives me the right?" Remember that John 1:12 says, "…
[A]s many as received Him. To them He gave the right to
become the children of God." You have been given that

right. It is now up to you to use it,

This applies not only in the area of financial prosperity. You can do the same when you need healing in your body, in your mind, emotions, relationships or any other area of life where there is lack. You should not accept lack in any area. It is up to you whether you accept things as they are or reach for the very best. That is what God promised, but you must receive - lay hold of it.

Verbal Habits Matter

You must be diligent about the words you speak in the everyday circumstances of life. Your words set the atmosphere in your life and could undermine everything you consciously desire. The words you speak at your relaxed and unguarded moments are important.

During a visit to Washington, DC several years ago I encountered a snow storm which bound me over an extra day. When the weather finally subsided, I caught a cab to the airport. The cab driver I hailed turned out to be a woman in her sixties. I was surprised that she was a cab driver at all, not to mention driving in the heavy snow of the storm's aftermath. We struck up a conversation and she began to describe her unwillingness to drive during the storm. Apparently cab drivers can make a lot of money if they are willing to take the risk in difficult or dangerous weather. She then said these words which I will never forget. "I am not about to drive in a storm to make some extra money. I was born poor, and I'm gonna die poor."

I was so amazed that she could say that about herself, I had to ask her where she got that expression. She had been saying it since she was a child. I remember thinking to myself, "And you have exactly what you have been confessing all these years" The Scripture says, "Death and life are in the power of the tongue." (Proverbs 18:21) The word power in that text is the Hebrew word "yad" which literally means the open hand. That is the hand which gives and receives. The tongue has the power to give and receive life, depending upon what you say.

The woman in my story had spent a lifetime speaking death into her life. Speaking "death" with your tongue does not mean you or someone else will physically drop dead at hearing your words. "Death" refers in this context to all that separates, denigrates, destroys, erodes, decomposes and degenerates. We invite "death" into our lives in everyday conversation with phrases such as: "It killed me" – "I could have died"-"I'm always broke" – "I can't" – "They won't let me" - "Things never go right for me" – "Don't get your hopes up" - "You can't win" – "What's the use in trying?" - "There's never enough money" – "I'm always coming down with something" – "I can't help it" – "There's no way" – "I'm getting old" - "I never remember names" - "I'm not very smart." "Murphy's Law - whatever can go wrong, will go wrong." etc. Banish such statements.

Humility is acknowledging that you are not the source of the power which brings success. God is the source. You are simply the conduit, the vessel into which that power flows. He has said that wealth and riches are in your house.

Why would you confess poverty? You may say, "Because I am poor." Then you are not walking by faith. Faith says, "even if I do not actually possess it physically, I confess what God's word says I have." I may feel sick in my body, but my confession is, "By His stripes I was healed." (2 Peter 2:24) Even if my body is racked with pain, I release the power that is in God's word. I do not wait until there is a manifestation of healing to acknowledge my healing.

The Apostle Thomas heard of the resurrection of Jesus from his fellow Apostles, he said, "Unless I see in His hands the print of the nails, and put my finger into the print of the nails, and put my hand into His side, I will not believe." (John 20:25) When Jesus appeared to them again, He said to Thomas, "Reach your finger here, and look at My hands; and reach your hands here, and put it into My side. Do not be unbelieving, but believing... Thomas, because you have seen Me, you have believed. Blessed are those who have not seen and yet have believed." (John 20:27,29)

The world says "I'll believe it when I see it." God says, "First believe it and then you will see it." You cannot wait until you experience your healing. Confess it now, then you will experience it. The same is true with financial prosperity. You cannot wait until you have wealth to stop saying you are poor. Stop saying it now, and start confessing abundance. Make up your mind this day that you will never speak a word inconsistent with the life God promises. Your words must be consistent with the wonderful vision you have for your life, and that vision must be based on the Word of God.

Beware of religious practices which rob the word of its power. Early in my ministry I was pastor of a traditional church. A well meaning Deacon who assisted me would often say: "Heavenly Father, tear the pastor down where he needs to be torn down." I would wince every time I heard that. Finally, I explained to him that God is not interested in tearing people down; the devil does that. God wants to build us up. The Deacon understood perfectly and ceased that prayer.

Imagine someone praying constantly that God would tear you down, for your own good of course. There is a great amount of that kind of traditional, formulaic and frankly dangerous expression going on in churches all over America. It is very misguided. If you are in a Church where poverty is considered virtue, sickness is a lesson from God and tragedy is God's way of maturing you, I have two words for you. Get out! That church will derail you from the destiny God has for you. Don't let that happen!

The Abundant Life
Does Not Happen Overnight

The physical universe operates according to very stable laws. It follows that the non-physical word - the world of the supernatural - operates according to very stable laws. These laws are spiritual, not physical. Jesus taught us that the Word of God is seed, and you are the sower. He said, "The sower sows the word." (Mark 4:14) That word then bears fruit, "...some thirty-fold, some sixty, and some a hundred." (Mark 4:20) The fruit of the words coming out of your mouth are how you live. Proverbs 18:20 says, "A man's stomach shall be satisfied from the fruit of his mouth.; From the produce of his lips he shall be filled." Proverbs 13:2 says, "A man shall eat well by the fruit of his mouth."

A tree bears fruit based on the seed from which the tree grew. You are the sower of seed in your own life. If you are picking bad fruit, it is because you have sown bad seed. If you want to start picking good fruit, start sowing good seed with the words of your mouth. Proverbs 18:21 says "death and life are in the power of the tongue, And those who love it will eat it's fruit." To "love" it is to understand that the tongue, used properly, is your friend. Wielded carelessly and thoughtlessly, it is a deadly enemy. Our words are critically important. They are powerful, and will either work for us or against us. David was a man after God's own heart, and he prayed, "Set a guard, O Lord, over my mouth; Keep watch over the door of my lips." (Psalm 141:3)

Many Christians fail to receive from God because they are waiting on God to "come down" to help them. God has already come down to help us all in the person of Jesus Christ. Romans 10:6-8 warns against this kind of thinking:"But the righteousness of faith speaks in this way, "Do not say in your heart, 'Who will ascend into heaven?'" (that is, to bring Christ down from above) or, "Who will descend into the abyss?" (that is, to bring

Christ up from the dead). But what does it say? "The word is near you, in your mouth and in your heart" (that is, the word of faith which we preach) God has put power in your tongue. He fully supports your confession. He wants you to be successful.

5

5TH PRINCIPLE

"Write It"

You must write down your goals. When Jesus faced His arch enemy on the mountain of temptation, He was confronted with ancient power which had brought mankind to its knees. Jesus Christ, the very Son of the Living God was God Himself. Yet when He responded to Satan, He did not invoke His Eternal Godhead. He used a different, but very powerful weapon embodied in three words: "It is written."

When Satan said, "If you are the Son of God, command that these stones become bread." Jesus answered, "IT IS WRITTEN, Man shall not live by bread alone, but by every word that proceeds from the mouth of God." [my emphasis]

Satan then took Him up on a the pinnacle of the temple, and said, "If you are the Son of God, throw yourself down, for it is written: 'He shall give His angels charge over you...Lest you dash your foot against a stone.'"

Jesus answered, "IT IS WRITTEN again, 'You shall not tempt the Lord your God.'" [my emphasis]

Then Satan took Jesus up on "an exceedingly high

mountain and showed Him all the kingdoms of the world and their glory" and said, "All these things I will give You if You will fall down and worship me."

Jesus answered, "Away with you Satan! For IT IS WRITTEN, 'You shall worship the Lord your God, and Him only you shall serve.'" [my emphasis] (Matthew 4:2-10)

Jesus answered Satan the same way again and again. "Then the devil left Him..." The WRITTEN WORD drove him off. It also drew friendly forces to Jesus aid. "[A]ngels came and ministered to Him."

The written word has power that calls forth angels and drives off demons. God's Word is not only spoken, but written. The Word is written by God's commandment. When John sees the glorified Christ, he is told, "I am Alpha and Omega. The First and the Last...What you see, WRITE in a book..." (Revelation 1:11) God instructs John eight times - in Revelation Chapters one, two and three - to "write." It is interesting to note that at the opening of Jesus ministry and the New Testament Scriptures, Jesus emphasis is on the written word.

At the close of those scriptures in the book of Revelation the emphasis is on the written word. Jesus says, "I am Alpha and Omega..." the first and last letters in the Greek alphabet. Jesus is saying among other things, "I am the written word." The Prophet Habakkuk received the same instruction as the Apostle John. Habakkuk said, "I will stand my watch...to see what He will say to me...Then the Lord answered me and said, 'WRITE the vision And make it plain on tablets that he may run who reads it.'" (Habakkuk 2:1,2)

Scientists have made much of the fact that chimpanzees have been trained to use sign language. Some take this as proof that primates have language capability. It is amazing the lengths to which people will go to prove what is so palpably false. The ability to make sounds which serve to communicate complex ideas is an astounding thing, almost supernatural in itself. Equally remarkable is the ability to reduce those sounds to written symbols universally understood and capable of conveying ideas. To suggest that all this is an accident of evolution belies the miraculous power of language.

There is an unfathomable gulf between humans and all other creatures because creation was designed that way. No amount of time or theorizing will ever bridge that gulf. Only one creature was made to represent the genius of Divinity.

We Write Because God Writes

Not only does God instruct that His servants "write", but God Himself writes. On the momentous occasion of giving the law to Moses, we are told, "And when He had made an end of speaking with him on Mt. Sinai, He gave Moses two tablets of the Testimony, tablets of stone, WRITTEN with the finger of God." (Exodus 31:18) "... The tablets were written on both sides; on the one side and on the other they were written. Now the tablets were the work of God, and the writing was the writing of God engraved on the tablets." (Exodus 32:15,16) Writing things down is so important to God that He personally wrote His law for man, but it goes further than that.

Writing gives certainty to the thought or idea which is expressed. When I practiced law, I often frustrated clients by requiring that all important agreements be set forth in writing. This is not to discount honorable people for whom a handshake is sufficient. The honor between people does not change the fact that writing an agreement gives it certainty. What if the person dies or becomes incapacitated? Her heirs may feel no obligation to honor an agreement for which there is no written documentation. If that agreement is in writing however, it transcends changes in circumstances, even the death of one or both parties. A written agreement can be passed on to heirs.

The same is true in the realm of the supernatural. God says, "Have I not WRITTEN to you excellent things of counsels and knowledge that I may make you know the CERTAINTY of the words of truth. That you may answer words of truth to those who send to you?" (Proverbs 22:20,21) God has written His wisdom to us that we may know with certainty that the things He has said and promised cannot fail. They will be fulfilled. Jesus said, "Heaven and earth will pass away, but My words will by no means pass away."(Matthew 24:35)

Six Reasons to Write it Down

1. To Establish the importance of what you desire.

God says "Have I not written to you excellent things…" The word "excellent" means "important, great and significant. God establishes the importance of His Word by writing it down. Writing memorializes – preserves – the value of what is said and thought.

When students graduate, they receive more than a handshake. Their accomplishment is recognized with a written document called a "degree." It is placed on parchment paper to assure that it will stand the test of time. It will be as clear and readable at the end of the graduate's long life as it was at graduation. That degree is an achievement intended to serve the graduate for a lifetime. It is too "important" to be left as a verbal expression. It is conferred in writing. On the other hand, if you enter into some minor transaction at a local store, occasionally you are handed a receipt, and asked, "Do you want this?"

I used to,say "No, I don't need it." I thought those minor purchases were not "important" enough for me to document in writing. I changed my mind about that when on a couple of occasions I found that I had been overcharged. Without that written document, I would not have known. Now I always take the receipt and look at it to be sure that it accurately reflects my purchase. I have even gone to the bank and found that the deposit receipt was not accurate and reflected an amount that was significantly less than what had been deposited. Without that written record, it might have been more difficult to retrace the transaction based on human memory.

Who would consider buying a house with all of the documents and complexity that entails, and put nothing in writing. In fact, the law will not allow you to do that. The "parole evidence" rule says that all real estate transactions must be in writing to be enforceable. Your dream home is not yours until it is documented in writing.

Your dream, your vision, your fondest hopes for your life must be put in writing. If they are truly important, put pen to paper or computer keys to document. You need not be a Hemingway to do this. Write down your vision and goals with every bit of accuracy you can muster. Keep adding details as time goes on. Continue building on your vision. What you desire out of life is very important. The person who is not disciplined enough to write down his vision is probably not disciplined enough to bring it to fruition. That is why investors always want a business plan. If the entrepreneur is not able to put that vision in writing, he will probably never turn it into bricks and mortar.

This is true not simply for business or career matters. On more than one occasion, I have taught the principles for finding the right mate. I have told searching singles to write down what they desire in a mate, in detail: height, weight, character, qualities, likes, dislikes, hobbies, career, etc. Those who have actually done that eventually come back to me saying, "I did it, and here is the man (or the woman) I was looking for." Is finding the right person an important goal of your life? Write it down! I should also mention as a footnote that writing down such important details prepares you to reject counterfeits. Many a wrong relationship would have been avoided had one or both parties been clear on what they were looking for.

2. To allow you to return to it again and again for prayer and reflection.

God says He has written "counsels and knowledge." The counsel and knowledge of God is of such that breadth and depth that understanding requires returning to it again and again. Having it in writing makes that possible.

It is almost impossible to study shifting verbal expressions which are ever changing with time. When there is one consistent document, you can study every word, every phrase and every verse. You can compare translations with each other and with the original language. Preachers and teachers may put their own gloss and emphasis on the text, but they can and must continue to return to the primary source, the Scripture itself. This not only provides for consistent study, but is also insurance against flights of fancy and heretical teaching.

A contract offers the same advantage. It is insurance against the changing perceptions and faulty memories of people. When there is some question or dispute, they return to what the contract says. When judges face a question of law, they have recourse to what the statute says. They can study the language, and it is always the same. Appellate judges render opinions in writing, and other judges can go back and analyze those opinions to study and compare one opinion with another. Writing provides the consistency necessary for stability in the pursuit of truth.

This principle works for your vision and goals. You want to be able to review, update and refine them. They will evolve. Goals will be achieved, and new goals will be established. Some goals will be dropped and replaced with others. There is a constant process of refinement which takes place over the years. Yet you will always be marching toward your vision. Having your vision written down maintains focus. Having your goals written down maintains momentum. It serves as a reminder to you to keep going.

3. To provide a basis for measuring one's knowledge.

God says, "that I might make you know." Knowing involves depth. To "know" in Scripture refers to intimacy. It is analogous to intimacy on the physical level. To know on this level is to have that knowledge buried deep within you.

Writing truth down makes it precise and repeatable for the purpose of knowing that truth. There is no "wiggle" room or lack of clarity. It is "certain".

That certainty created by writing it down allows you to immerse your mind and heart in it, over and over again which is a key to bringing it to pass in your life.

4. To provide an unchanging reality.

God says He has written, "to make you know the certainty." Once it is written, it is certain; it does not change. There is an abiding stability in writing. We can read ancient texts read by people hundreds, even thousands of years ago. Those [words] take on an unchanging nature once they are written. A written contract, a written statute, a written legal opinion, all serve the same function. They cannot be changed. The only thing that can happen is to write something which supersedes what was already written. Yet even when that is done, the original document continues. If this is true for man-made documents, it is much more true for the Word of God. God's Word is like Him, "the same yesterday, today, and forever."(Hebrews 13:6) Indeed God is inseparable from His Word. He and His Word are One. "In the beginning was the Word, and the Word was with God, and the Word was God." (John 1:1)

Your vision must have an unchanging quality. It may be adjusted and refined, but there must be a concrete core which can withstand the shifting sands of time. That stability allows the vision to be relentlessly pursued. Your vision may be to run a fortune 500 company. Whether you build that company yourself or you are hired by a board of directors to run an existing corporation may change as your career unfolds. You must stay focused on the vision, meditating it and incubating it. Then even those events which seem to be against it will work for you in ways you could not have planned consciously.

5. To provide a treasure which can be rehearsed and stored in the memory.

God says "that you may answer words of truth..." This is very similar to the admonishment of Peter to "always be ready to give a defense to everyone who asks you a reason for the hope that is in you..." (1 Peter 3:15) In order to be "always ready," what is written must be stored in your own mind and heart. That is very difficult to do without a record from which the mind can draw precise information to be stored for some future time. It would be difficult to learn a song if every time you hear it the song has changed. Your mind will not know what phrases and rhymes to accept. Nor will you be able to convey that song to others. You cannot convey what is not clear in your own mind. Writing it down provides a clarity for the mind to grasp and store.

Memorize your vision. If it is a building, memorize its dimensions, interior decorations and exterior design. See it clearly and constantly. When the opportunity arises to discuss it, be ready to give a reason for the hope you have to bring it to pass. When opportunity comes for you to advance your vision, you do not want to have to say, "Wait, let me go get my notes." You want to be ready at all times.

6. To provide a means for measuring and verifying progress and fulfillment.

Part of knowing with certainty the words of truth is being able to measure progress and fulfillment. That can only be done when there is an accurate written record of what has been said. Seven Hundred years before the coming of Jesus Christ, the Prophet Isaiah said, "Behold, the virgin shall conceive and bear a Son and shall call His name Immanuel." (Isaiah 7:14)

We can now verify the accuracy of that statement in light of what happened two thousand years ago. Had it not been written 700 years before the birth of Jesus Christ, there would have been a debate about whether Isaiah actually said it. No reasonable person can deny that this scripture was fulfilled in the birth of the Christ Child. Some scholars try to raise questions, but the text is so plain that their nitpicking objections ring hollow. The accuracy of the Scriptures has been demonstrated in the lives of millions of people over the last two millennia. His birth, ministry, trial, crucifixion, death, entry into hell and His glorious resurrection were all prophesied hundreds of years before they occurred. We can verify that this is so because "it is written."

You need to write down your vision and goals so that you can measure progress and fulfillment. The singles I mentioned earlier were later able to go back to their written descriptions of the ideal mate and compare it to the mate they got. They were amazed at the staggering accuracy of their description. You want the same kind of experience. You want to see your written vision come to fulfillment right before your very eyes, and it will.

God Writes Everything Down

Keep in mind that the premise of all that you have learned so far is that you are a unique creation of God, made to be like Him. Therefore you are endowed with the supernatural ability to function as He does, except in finite measure. God is infinite in power; we are finite in power. The power which derives from God's supernatural realm or kingdom, however, is far more potent than the power that exists in the natural realm of the flesh. God has shared with us the tools that He uses. For example, do you realize that God writes everything you do? He keeps an ongoing "journal" out of which He will judge every human being. Jesus said, "...[F]or very idle word men may speak, they will give account of it in the day of judgment." (Matthew 12:36) The Apostle John, in the Revelation said, "And I saw the dead, small and great, standing before God, and books were opened...And the dead were judged according to their works, by the things which were written in the books." (Revelation 20:12) The judgment of God will be absolutely fair and just because nothing will be left out, not a single detail. There will be no disputing the record. It will be completely accurate.

One way of experiencing the power of this principle is to establish a journal which allows you to record your life: dreams, prayers, vision, goals and experiences. "Journaling" is a very powerful tool of progress. Through it you can keep track of your life in a way your memory alone will never allow. A journal is an accurate way of reviewing how you were perceiving things at the time you wrote and how accurate your perception was as you look at it in hindsight. It also provides a wonderful way of assessing your thoughts, words and deeds. Seeing yourself more accurately helps you to improve yourself more effectively. The scripture says, "For if we would judge ourselves, we would not be judged." (1 Corinthians 11:31)

Not only does God write down everything we do, but each human being is written in the Lamb's Book of Life. Each of us has what you might call an "existence certificate" in heaven. I did not say "birth" certificate because that would not include all the unborn children whose lives are recorded. The common perception is that people's names are added to the Book of Life when they become saved. Actually, the scripture teaches that all our names are in the Book of Life, and names are "blotted out" when they are judged without Christ. Jesus said, "He who overcomes... I will not blot out his name from the Book of Life..." (Revelation 3:5) And further, it says, "... if anyone takes away from the words of the book of this prophecy, God shall take away his part from the Book of Life." (Revelation 21:19) If you are an unsaved person reading this book, your name is in the Book of Life, but it will not remain there unless you receive Jesus Christ as your Lord and Savior.

Why would God do it this way? It is not God's will or plan that anyone be lost. The Book of Life was written before the foundation of the world. God's plan was that every person born would come to Him. Every human being who would ever live was made for God's love and fellowship. Every person's name was recorded for heaven. We cannot blame God for human rejection of His offer of love. When human beings die without forgiveness of their sins through Christ, their names are blotted out. For those who receive Christ, their names can never be blotted out. It is an eternally written record.

God is so intricate in His plan and love for each person that the design and detail of our being was written down before time and history began, certainly before we ever existed. Psalm 139:16 says, "Your eyes saw my substance, yet being unformed. And in your book they were all written, the days fashioned for me, when as yet there were none of them." God had a vision of who you were to be. That vision was one of health, wealth, grace and glory. You represent the crown jewel of His creative work. That vision for you and your life came out of the depths of God's being. It could only be good. Having "seen" you within Himself, He wrote down what He saw.

Why then are human beings not the majestic God-like creatures we were made to be, full of love, virtue and awesome supernatural power to do good? The answer is that sin polluted us and introduced death. The Father sent Jesus to restore His original plan of glory for His children. Nonetheless, each of us is free to ignore God's marvelous plan, and sadly, most do.

I hazard to guess what percentage of those who read this book will actually follow through to put its principles to work. Ten percent may have the discipline, commitment and interest to follow through. You be the one in ten whose life is transformed. You make the decision to "choose" prosperity over poverty, health over sickness, joy over sorrow and success over failure. That is God's will for you, but you must make the choice.

Keep in mind that the whole cosmos has been made imperfect – wounded – by sin.

In the first edition of this book, I made this statement:

"It is the principle of sin, rebellion against God and His truth which has brought about birth defects and other destructive natural occurrences."

It is a benign declaration that every Bible believing Christian understands. Little did I know at the time that five years later, I would win the Republican nomination for Lt. Governor of Virginia. That put me in the media spotlight as I had never been. The mainstream media has a refined antipathy for Bible believing Christians. Needless to say, they were incensed over comments I made about homosexuality prior to running for office. Of course, those comments were made in the context of sermons or interviews on Christian media. I said nothing to be ashamed of because my answers were true. I later came to realize that my comments while true were not always wise. We'll come back to that.

In an effort to smear and disqualify me from high office, the media took the "birth defects" statement out of context and reported that I said that if a child is born with disabilities or birth defects, it is because the parents sinned. They completely ignored the sentence before it:

"the whole cosmos has been made imperfect – wound – by sin."

   Most Christians with a modicum of biblical understanding know that I was not blaming parents for their children's disabilities. I was making a reference to the doctrine of original sin. Birth defects and all other problems originate in the fallenness of mankind. There is no one to one correlation - at least in most cases - to someone's sin and the terrible problems that plague us in life. In other words, children are not born with birth defects because their parents committed sin. It was preposterous to even suggest that I believe otherwise. It is sad that journalists charged with promulgating facts and truth would stoop to that kind of slander. If they are that ignorant of biblical references, they should not purport to write about the subject matter. If they do such things out of bias, knowing that their narrative is untrue, they are dangerous to a Constitutional Republic.

   Back to the point, none of us reflects the perfection God originally intended. Since the fall of Adam and Eve, we are all "born in sin and shaped in iniquity." We inherit that condition, not because of something our mothers and fathers did, but because of what Adam and Eve did.

   In spite of that unhappy fact, we still bear the mark of our Creator. Your genetic code is the handwriting of God, written before you existed. Even though that writing has been marred by sin, our genetic blueprint is proof of the existence of God and His infinite intelligence, purpose and design.

The writing of God is even more intimate than we imagine. Not only has He written about us, God has written on us. God says, "I will put My law in their mind and write them on their hearts; and I will be their God and they shall be My people." (Hebrews 8:10) It is awesome to contemplate that our very being bears the signature of God. We have the love letter of God, not merely sent to us, but written within us. There can be no more intimate touch. His Spirit has written the language of His love on your spirit. There is Spirit to spirit intimacy between God and His own. His character, His morals, His gifts, His love, joy and peace are written within you. You have the very "spiritual DNA" of God in you. He wrote our physical "members" before the world was, but He also wrote on our spirits. That means that every fiber of our being -visible and invisible, inward and outward – has been written by God.

Writing Establishes Law

There is no such thing as law that is not written down, at least not in civilized countries. Written law gives notice to those who are bound by that law. In a sense, the law is never really broken. It breaks those who try to break it. Either they are caught and pay the price required or they spend their lives trying to hide from the consequences of their actions. The law does not change because people refuse to adhere to it. By its nature it stands against all efforts to stop its fulfillment.

When God wrote your name in His Book of Life, He established law. When you write your vision, you establish law in your domain.

Writing is the First Step of Manifestation

There is one very important aspect of the principle of "writing it" which I must discuss. When you write down a thought or idea, a vision or dream, you transfer it from the realm of the non-material into the realm of the material. It is not fulfilled at that point, but the process has begun. An architect envisions a great structure. He has it in his mind and in his heart. But it is left in the world of the non-material. The moment he puts pencil to paper, it has a form of tangible existence, without which it can never become a building. It must first be written.

A contract originates as an idea shared between two or more people. While they are discussing their agreement, it is just an idea with no force or ability to enforce it in the legal world. Once that idea is reduced to a written agreement – a contract – it has the force of law behind it. Before any other tangible action has been taken, that contract is tangible proof that the thing will be done or at least effort will be under way to get it done. This is the way it works in the natural, which is a shadow and reflection of the supernatural.

This will drive the point home. The Bible is not simply

a Book about God, written by God. The Bible is a manifestation of God Himself. It is God pouring Himself onto the written page. Everything He has written is true because He is Truth. Everything that is written must come to pass. Not one word can fail because He is Almighty and cannot fail. What you write of your vision, faith, hope and expectations is a manifestation of you; it comes out of your inner depths as dynamic creativity and it has power. That creative power was placed in you by your Creator, that you might reflect His image. Use that power.

6

6TH PRINCIPLE

"Meditate It"

I addressed this subject in my first book, never expecting that I would run for office and that reporters and my opponent would go through it with a fine tooth comb hoping to find some avenue of attack. If you are looking for a way to hurt people, you will always find it. This book is about putting yourself in a position to help yourself and others. It is the sad reality of politics today that people who are supposed to be neutral in the political debate are in fact advocates for a particular side, namely the secularist, atheist left.

I could never have anticipated the things they would light on because their attack was not based on reality, but distortion. I realize it was only a reflection of their own warped thinking and disdain for Christians. We love them anyway.

This was the brief small statement that was distorted by the media to obscure the point I was making, but most importantly to depict me as a bizarre figure:

"When one hears the word meditation it conjures up an image of Maharishi Yoga talking about finding a mantra and striving for nirvana."

That was a tongue in cheek reference to following a guru "Maharishi Yoga" not a reference to yoga exercises. "The proper spelling of the name is Maharishi Yogi, but it was an attempt at light humor. The press ignored the Maharishi part which is the name of a guru, and focused on the "Yoga" which clearly was not a reference to exercises at all. Of course, based on what followed, political adversity took a flight of fancy and promoted the false story that in my book, I tell people that if you do yoga exercises, you are demon possessed. It is hard to imagine that any person who can read would be that incapable of understanding a simple sentence. The problem of course was not intelligence but intentions. I must diverge for a moment here to speak to the person reading this book who may not understand. Christians are not against yoga exercise. Many use it. One of my daughters, a wonderful Christian, loves it. One of the ministers in my church is a yoga instructor. When I ran for office, the press had a field day with that one sentence. If you are unfamiliar with how vicious politics can be and the ways in which opponents smear you, this probably seems silly. Frankly, it is ridiculous, but when the press paints a dishonest caricature of a person to defeat him or her politically, it is corrupt and despicable.

What exactly do I believe? I do believe that Christians should stay away from forms of eastern meditation which deal with emptying oneself. We do not empty ourselves. We want to be filled with the word of God and the Spirit of God. Yoga as an exercise is fine, but the spiritual aspects of it should be eschewed.

While non-Christian meditation may seem to have certain physical and mental benefits, it also has potential hazards which outweigh the benefits. From a strictly Christian perspective, the universe is not a spiritual vacuum. It has two diametrically opposing forces. God, who is infinitely good. The other is Satan, who is completely corrupt and diabolical. God will never force himself on anyone. If you do not invite Him into your life, He will not intrude. Satan on the other hand has no respect for human autonomy. He is happy to invade your life and take control.

People serve Satan without any conscious decision. The drug dealer serves Satan. The gangster, the pornographer and any other purveyors of immoral services also serve the devil. In most cases of course, they have engaged in no ritual or selling of their souls. When you dedicate your life to an activity which hurts human beings or turns them into slaves, you have in effect sold your soul to the devil.

To be sure, eastern forms of meditation are not the equivalent of drug dealing or gangster activity. That is not the point I am making. The point is that Satan does not need a conscious commitment to take control of a person's life. He only needs an open vessel. He needs no invitation. He is happy to invade. What people allow to occupy their minds is what controls them. We should be conscious of that and choose wisely. Philippians 4:8 says, "...whatever things are true, whatever things are noble, whatever things are just, whatever things are pure, whatever things are lovely, whatever things are of good report, if there is any virtue and if there is anything praiseworthy—meditate on these things." That is very good advice.

Christians should meditate on the Word of God - the Bible. It speaks to every realm of life. God said to Joshua as he was about to embark on the battle to possess the promised land, "This Book of the Law shall not depart from your mouth, but you shall meditate in it day and night, that you may observe to do all that is written in it. For then you will make your way prosperous, and then you will have good success." (Joshua 1:8) This is a promise.

God says to Joshua, in effect, "Fill yourself up on My promises." He does not say, "If you do this, I will prosper you." Rather he says to Joshua, "If you do this, YOU will MAKE YOUR WAY PROSPEROUS." He tells Joshua that his destiny is in his own hands. God is the Supreme Authority, but He delegates to Joshua the key to his own success or failure. This is very different than what we often hear. Trust in God and He will do these things for you. But this text says trust in God, in His word, and you will be able to do these things for yourself. The "promised land" of the Old Covenant was a gift to the children of Israel. Yet God placed the power to possess the land in the hands of a man. God has a "promised land" for you, but He has placed in your hands the power to enter in and possess the land.

Everyone wants to prosper and have good success, but not every one is willing to pay the price to get it. We want to succeed on our jobs, in our businesses, in our marriages, as parents and in every other area of life. God knew that Joshua wanted to succeed. After all, he was stepping into the shoes of Moses, one of the greatest figures in history.

God does not do it for him, but He tells him how to do it. God knows that you want to succeed, but He will not do it for you. He tells you how to do it.

If you have been stuck in the past, held down by past failures, it is time to break lose. Everyone meditates. The problem is what you are meditating. If you think often about past disappointments and perceived failures, real or imagined slights, you are definitely meditating. Meditation has creative power, but you may be creating the wrong thing.

The Apostle Paul was a man whose authority was often questioned because of his scandalous background as a persecutor of the Church. He presided over the execution of Christians, and thought of himself as a hero for doing so. That was "Saul". That dark past could have haunted him all his life if he had allowed it to define him. He had an answer to living in the past and refusing to let go. He said, "forgetting those things which are behind and reaching forward to those things which are ahead, I press toward the goal for the prize of the upward call of God in Christ Jesus." (Philippians 3:13,14)

Some married people are living together in an "unholy" state of matrimony because they are unable to move beyond the past. Careers are stagnated because people filled with potential are held back by past disappointments. People with wonderful ideas never pursue them because they have experienced failure in the past. Whole groups of people fail to realize their potential because they are stuck in the mental and emotional quagmire of past oppression. They are so busy looking at the past, they cannot make the most of the present and future. Individuals and groups can be shackled by the chains of their own obsession with the past. Those mental chains can be just as real as any forged with iron or steel.

The lie that you cannot rise above your past will enslave you, but the truth that God has a wonderful plan for you can set you free.

Meditation Defined

All human beings "meditate." One form of meditation is worry, anxious thinking. While it is often unconscious it can have immense negative effects. The so called "bad luck" some people have is sometimes the result of this mental habit which leads to bad decisions.

It can take the form of constant regret over decisions of the past that cannot be changed: "If only I had. If only it hadn't." This kind of thinking leads only to frustration, and robs us of hope for the future. You cannot change the past, but you can make different choices today that will lead to different outcomes tomorrow.

Another form it can take is, "Why me? Why did this happen to me? What did I do to deserve this?" This leads to self doubt and failure to recognize the good things we have in our lives. Frankly, there are some events in life that I believe will remain a mystery until we get to the other side. By that time it won't matter. We will be so overwhelmed with the joy and peace of being with God that things we thought were so important, will fade into insignificance.

The other very negative form meditation can take is, "I can't. I can't do it because I am black. I can't do it because I'm poor. I can't do it because I'm a woman. I can't do it because I am handicapped. I can't do it because they won't let me. I can't do it because of my lack of education." On and on it goes. That kind of thinking turns the normal challenges of life into insurmountable obstacles.

When you allow yourself to think in these unproductive ways, you create hopelessness. Such people are indeed held back, but not by others. They are holding themselves back. As an American of African descent, it never ceases to amaze me how slavery and Jim Crow segregation are still used as explanations for the lack of progress in the black community in America. What young people need is a message of hope, not despair. When they are constantly told by so called leaders that their circumstances are the result of slavery and "systemic racism," it should come as no surprise that they turn to gangs and drug dealing as a way to survive and eke out an existence. They need instead to be reminded of the enviable position they are in as Americans. People around the world are desperate to get here because of the opportunities our country affords those who are willing to work hard.

No doubt we all wish slavery and segregation had never happened, but they did. The subjugation of people is still going on in the world, particularly in some Muslim countries where non-Muslims are being pressed into slavery and women are treated like second class citizens.

This behavior ultimately has nothing to do with race and everything to do with the sinful nature of human beings. For that reason, it will continue. However, slavery in America ended 150 years ago. Segregation ended 50 years ago. At some point the shelf life on those historical events will run out, and it will no longer be possible to use them as excuses for bad personal choices. To tell a whole generation of people their condition is the result of what someone else is doing and that there is no hope until they stop doing it, is to lock them in a mental cell. They will never escape because they have become their own jailers.

Of course they've had help constructing their own mental prison. When some of us say, "you can unlock the door to your future," we are vilified as a sell-outs out who do not understand their "oppression." I understand it perfectly. That's why I tell them the truth. Truth liberates. Lies enslave. If you meditate on lies, you may feel absolved of responsibility for your condition, but you have consigned yourself to a life sentence of misery and mediocrity. If you meditate on the truth, the truth will make you free.

One of the procedures for studying the effect of new drugs is double blind studies. This involves giving the drug to one group and giving a placebo (a sugar pill) to the second group. Both groups believe that they are receiving the actual drug. This way they determine how much of supposed effects are psychological and which are the actual effects of the drug. Here is the first interesting result. In some studies as much as forty percent of those who get the placebo experience improved health. This is because of their profound belief and meditation that they are being helped by the drug, even though they are not actually getting it.

The double blind study means that not only are the recipients unaware that they are getting a placebo, but the Doctor who dispenses the pill is also unaware that some participants are getting a placebo. Another "control" mechanism in these studies is that one Doctor is told which patients are getting the placebo and another is not. The result is that patients of the Doctor who thinks that they are all getting the real medicine do better than the patients of the Doctor who knows they are not. The simple point is that the Doctor's thinking has an impact on the patients. If she thinks her patients will do better, they do, even though the basis for that belief is false. If the Doctor thinks they will not do better, their progress mirrors her expectations.

That is how powerfully the thoughts of human beings can affect the tangible. Christians should always meditate on the positive and uplifting truths of the Bible and the promises of God it sets forth.

Jim Carey, long before he became the famous comedian, wrote himself a check for $20 million. He kept that check in his wallet, and took it out to look at it every day until the day he was paid $20 million for a movie. Carey was meditating on his dream of becoming a successful comedian.

There are two words in the Hebrew scriptures translated meditation. One is "*hagah*" which means "to ponder or study." This is the word used in Joshua 1:8. The other is the word "*siyach*", which means "to converse with or talk to oneself ". The New Covenant also has two words in the Greek. One is "*meletao*" which means, "to revolve in the mind or imagine." The third is the word "*logizomai*", which means "to reckon, count, take inventory of or think on." Each of these words sets forth aspects of meditation.

Meditation in Practice

You may be facing financial challenges, and not know what to do. For strength and comfort turn to Deuteronomy 8:18, which says, "And you shall remember the Lord your God, for it is He who gives you power to get wealth, that He may establish His covenant which he swore to your fathers as it is this day." Open your Bible to that scripture and recite it again and again. You may focus on different aspects of it: "I must remember the Lord. The Lord gives me power. He gives me power to get wealth. He does this to establish his covenant with me." Each aspect of the verse or the whole of it is a fit subject for meditation when the need is for financial or other resources. This is not magic that will transform your life over night, but the principle behind it is true: YOUR OUTWARD LIFE IS GOING TO BE A REFLECTION OF YOUR INNER LIFE. The two are inextricably linked.

Notice in the above example, I made Deuteronomy 8:18 personal to me. God gives ME power to get wealth, that He may establish His covenant with ME. Based on God's promises you may be inspired to start a business. You can meditate on this scripture and what your business will look like when it is thriving and successful. You can see yourself paying the payroll, guiding and working with your employees and collecting your profits. Meditation allows your vision to grow. You begin to see it as if it already exists. "See" the new life you want to live. The happy family you want to have, the beautiful new home you want to live in. Until you can see a better life for yourself, you will never have one.

As the placebo drug test illustration shows, meditation is a powerful tool for physical healing. When you are sick, find healing scriptures to meditate. For example, 2 Peter 2:24 says by the stripes of Jesus, "you were healed." Your meditation might be "by His stripes, I was healed. That healing is working in my body now." Allow yourself to be filled with the joy of freedom from sickness. We are not talking about the power of positive thinking but the power of faith in God - faith in His love and desire to do you good. Sickness is not God's will for anyone. This is not to deny the reality of sickness or its presence in people's lives. The problem is that because of bad theology, Christians are often convinced that God wants them sick, that there is some kind of grand scheme in which the sickness is good for them. Jesus said, "I have come that they might have life." He did not say that He came to make anyone sick or cause anyone to die. Think about that.

God does take bad situations and use them to bring good things. That is what any good parent does. You do not will bad things for your children, but when they happen, you try to use them as life lessons and hope that your children emerge stronger and better. Because your child is victorious over a life threatening disease and comes out of the experience wiser and more mature does not mean that you wanted the illness to happen. You would rather your child learn lessons without the risk of death. God is no different.

God's word says in Jeremiah 29:11, "For I know the thoughts that I think toward you,...thoughts of peace and not of evil, to give you a future and a hope." Does that sound like God wants you sick? The point is to always meditate on what God wants for you, which is the very best that life has to offer. What about the person with physical handicaps and limitations? Never see your self as limited. We have all heard and seen amazing stories of people with severe handicaps who achieved extraordinary things.

As we discussed earlier, the ideas and beliefs which preoccupy your mind have a powerful impact on what happens to you in life. I'm convinced that much of what people call "bad luck" is really bad thinking. As we have seen, the person who believes he is taking real medicine gets better even though it is only a placebo. That is the power of the mind to impact the body.

Your meditation is a kind of placebo. You are taking constant doses of an alternate reality which at first only exists in the mind, but eventually has physical impact on you and helps shape the world around you. Your goal should be to make that meditation so real that it creates a faith reality that is more powerful than the physical reality. That meditation should be rooted and grounded in the Word of God because the Word of God is more than just words on a page. It is living and powerful. [Hebrews 4:12]

The word of God will also set you free from what some call "generational curses" - problems in a family that repeat from one generation to another. Meditation can help break the thought patterns that perpetuate the curse:

"My grandfather died young; my father died young and I will probably die young too."

"My grandmother died of cancer; my mother died of cancer, and cancer will probably get me too."

"My father died of alcoholism. All my brothers and sisters are alcoholics. I will probably be a drunk too."

Most people would not consciously say such things, but they think them and live in constant fear of repeating the destructive pattern of their parents.

A favorite scripture of mine is Psalm 91:16, "With long life I will satisfy him, and show him my salvation." Fullness of life is not simply a matter of length but of "satisfaction". There is no satisfaction in spending the last years of life in a vegetative state. Yet some people anticipate that result. If you think, speak and behave consistent with that expectation, the likelihood is that your body and mind will comply. Psalm 91:16 teaches a different outcome. So does Psalms 103:2-5, which says, Bless the Lord, O my soul, And forget not all His benefits: Who forgives all your iniquities, Who heals all your diseases, Who redeems your life from destruction, Who crowns you with loving kindness and tender mercies,

Who satisfies your mouth with good things, So that your youth is renewed like the eagle's.

It is also very unhealthy to allow hatred and bitterness toward others to become your meditation. The first victim of that kind of preoccupation is you. Never meditate on harming or seeking vengeance against others. Meditate on doing good and good will come to you. Meditate on doing evil and evil will come to you. Proverbs 4:23 says, "Keep your heart with all diligence, For out of it spring the issues of life." Guard your inner life by consciously and intentionally choosing to meditate only on what will enhance your life.

Here is a meditation which has worked for me. It is not a scripture quote, but it is based in scripture. "THE PROBLEMS WHICH COME TO ME ARE AN OPPORTUNITY FOR GOD TO SHOW HIS MIGHTY POWER IN ME AND TO MANIFEST HIS GLORY THROUGH ME." The primary passage from which that meditation is inspired is James 1:2-4, which says, "… Count it all joy when you fall into various trials, knowing that the testing of your faith produces patience. But let patience have its perfect work, that you may be perfect and complete, lacking nothing." God's plan is to demonstrate His power and glory in your behalf.

The end result is that you will lack nothing, which is to say that you will have everything that brings you satisfaction in life. Meditation on these truths will break through the hindrances thrown in your path.

Why Meditation Works

All of these principles work together to pull your dreams into fulfillment. It works, but why does it work?

First you must know exactly who you are as a being made in the image of God. Second Thessalonians 2:23 says that you are a spirit. You do not have a spirit; you ARE a spirit. You have a soul which is so intimately attached to your spirit that nothing can separate the two except the Word of God. [Hebrews 4:12] You possess and live in a body. When your body is dead, you will live on. The only question is where, whether with God in heaven or with Satan in an eternal lake of fire and torment. You may be thinking, "He sounds like some kind of fundamentalist." Let me help you understand heaven and hell. When you die, you become pure spirit capable of transcending time and space. As such you inherit potentially immense power. If you die an outlaw spirit, you cannot be permitted to roam free. You must be imprisoned. Can you imagine what it would be like if Hitler were permitted to roam as a spirit, influencing people and life. Satan and his demons are enough.

Ghosts are not people who have died and gotten caught between the two worlds as the entertainment world would have you think. They are demonic spirits seeking to put people in fear and bondage. The only prison for outlaw spirits – human and angelic - is the one constructed for the original outlaw spirit, Satan, once named Lucifer. That place is called hell or hades. Without Christ, that is where you go by choice. If you are a spirit submitted to God, you will live with Him in a place of eternal love, joy and peace. That place is heaven.

This body is simply the shell which you inhabit for the time being. God has promised through Christ that each believer in Him will receive a new resurrection body untouchable by sin or death ever again. We will return to this later. The Greek word for soul in the Bible is "*psuche*"– the personality. It is made up of the mind, will and emotions. Each of us has a unique personality. Each person's mind, will and emotions operate and incline differently than another's. The spirit on the other hand is the very life force which animates the human being. It is what was breathed into Adam which made him a living soul. It is the very nature of God himself, whereby we relate to God, spirit to Spirit. It is that part of us which is made for vital union with God. It is the core, the essential nature of who we are. However, when the connection with God was broken by sin, we became dead spirits, in union and league with God's enemy, Satan, and reflecting his personality rather than God's. What I am about to say is not intended to insult or condemn anyone, but it is hard truth which may not be easy to accept.

The reason why most people do not want to hear the gospel and do not like the so called "holy rollers", "Jesus fanatics", "Bible thumpers", etc. is that most people are dead spirits. As such they have the nature of Satan who does not want to have anything to do with God or anyone related to Him. Of course they are not aware that they are imbued with the nature of Satan. They would be mortified by the idea of being viewed as Satanists or devil worshipers. Satan benefits far more from people who do not know they serve him than from those who knowingly bow to him. Your spirit was made for attachment. It is either attached to God or to Satan, but it is not neutral, no matter how much people think themselves to be. A person may be good, moral and upright by all outward appearances. Nevertheless, all our "righteousness" is as filthy rags because apart from Him, it is nothing but self-righteousness. (Isaiah 64:6)

When the human spirit is disconnected from God, that is "spiritual death." God told Adam that he would die on the very day that he ate from the forbidden tree. Adam did not die physically until he was 930 years old, but he died spiritually the very moment he sinned. From that point Adam had a very different reaction to the presence of God. He ran. People are still running today. Once Adam took on the nature of his new lord, Satan, he reacted toward God the same way Satan does, with fear and loathing. It has become hatred for many even if they would never admit it. They hate churches, the very thing Christ died for. They hate preachers, His representatives. They do not believe the Bible because "it has been tampered with" or "it was written by one race of people to enslave another." They have a thousand excuses, but the underlying reality is disdain for God.

The nature of spiritual death is distaste for true spiritual life. Have you noticed the respect and awe people have for eastern philosophies and religions which reject the God of the Bible? When a Buddhist sets himself on fire in some misguided protest, the media does not condemn such fanaticism. But the same media readily caricature the entire Christian community based on the excesses of a few. Non-Christian religions have their own values which are often highly questionable. Yet there is a remarkable deference paid to any religious system that does not include Christ as the Son of God. Affinity for anything but what is truly of God is the nature of spiritual death.

Spiritual death does not involve the spirit going out of existence. Since it was created in the image of God, it is an eternal reality. You will never die in the sense of ending consciousness. People think that suicide is a way out of problems. Instead it is the way into greater horror and heartache than the finite human mind can fathom. If you have suffered from depression or contemplated suicide, banish those thoughts from your mind forever. Know that suicide, instead of making things better, will make them infinitely and eternally worse. The principles God gave us in His word will deliver you from being a victim of forces beyond your control.

The Spirit Should Dominate The Soul and Body

God sent His Holy Spirit to guide you. On the other hand, when the human the spirit is disconnected from God, the life is dominated by the desires of the flesh and the instability of emotions. Fleshly desires lead to a life of promiscuity, drug abuse, obesity and a host of other problems associated with satisfying the urges of the flesh. The soul – mind, will and emotions – with its egocentric focus will lead to a life of selfishness. The mantra of the soul is "Me First! Me Last! Me Only! Me always."

The soul is also the seat of the emotions. Emotions can be constructive or destructive. A woman thinks her husband is cheating on her because he stays out late in the evening. She follows him and learns that he leaves the apartment of another woman each night. She fills with rage at his betrayal and infidelity. Her mind races with the images of her husband in the intimate embrace of another woman. She loves him so much that life no longer seems worth living. She buys a gun with the intention of killing herself. On the evening, she plans do it, her husband comes home early. He walks in the door with a smile on his face, but she takes this as the ultimate show of arrogance. She confronts him, but he denies the accusation. In a fit of ultimate rage, she pulls the gun which she plans to use on her herself and turns it on her husband, shooting him dead. She then follows through with her plan to take her own life and fires a bullet into her own head. The investigation of the murder-suicide finds that the husband was having a portrait painted of himself as a surprise gift to his wife. It was something she had requested years earlier when they could not afford such extravagance. The wife was a victim of her emotions. Her feelings were so real, but they were so wrong.

Your emotions will say many things, much of it negative and discouraging. Do not listen. Fill your mind with meditation on what is good. "Whatever things are true, whatever things are noble, whatever things are just, whatever things are pure, whatever things are lovely, whatever things are of good report, if there is any virtue and if there is anything praiseworthy – meditate on these things." (Philippians 4:8)

The mantra of the body is "Pleasure! Pleasure! Pleasure!" Human beings often allow lust and desire for pleasure to dominate their lives. God's intent is that the human spirit would be led by the Holy Spirit. This relationship creates in us a desire for righteousness and holiness before God. When you walk in the Spirit of God, in agreement with and submission to Him, you do not fulfill the lusts of the flesh. (Galatians 5:16)

Feed Your Spirit

Your spirit feeds on and draws strength from the Word of God the way the body draws strength from physical food. The Word of God is fuel and energy for the human spirit in the same way that gasoline is energy and fuel for an automobile. A car cannot run without fuel. A human being cannot function without energy. Jesus said, "Man shall not live by bread alone, but by every word that proceeds from the mouth of God." (Matthew 4:4) Jesus is not denying that human beings need physical food to live in the natural world. He is saying that life has another, more important dimension. Physical food is temporal support for temporal life. The Word of God is eternal food for eternal life. Jesus asserted this truth again by saying, "He who eats this bread will live forever." (John 6:58) The words that I speak to you are spirit, and they are life." (John 6:58b, 63b)

Spiritual life begins – the human spirit comes alive– when you accept and believe the Word of God as truth. The Spirit of God uses God's Word to connect you to the will of God. It will strengthen your ability to create the life God intended for you. Jesus said, "I am the vine, you are the branches. He who abides in Me, and I in Him, bears much fruit; for without Me you can do nothing... If you abide in Me and My words abide in you, you will ask what you desire, and it shall be done for you." (John 15:5,7)

The life force that flows through you is the power of God Himself, and that power is in His Word. When the life of God is flowing in your life, you are supernaturally endowed to bear fruit. What fruit? Whatever you "desire". This presumes of course that your desire is informed by the Word of God. You then become an extension and expression of His will. Do not for a moment think that you are thereby limited or deprived. His plan for you has far more glory and grandeur than anything you can begin to imagine. "The blessing of the Lord makes one rich and He adds no sorrow with it." (Proverbs 10:22) For "...He is able to do the exceedingly abundantly above all that we ask or think." (Ephesians 3:20)

The fleshly life is the life of pleasure and self-gratification, making one the slave of the five senses and the physical circumstances of life. The "soulish" life is the life of the ego, making one the slave of one's own desires and emotions. It may involve a life of great physical discipline and denial, but its end is selfishness. The life of the spirit is the life submitted to God, making one the child and servant of God.

God Meditates

The creation of the universe involved meditation. God created by taking what was in Himself, meditating and speaking it into existence. Before God spoke, He meditated. Everything God created came from within Him. Take a fresh look at a familiar scripture. Genesis 1:2 says, "And the Spirit of God was hovering over the face of the waters." The word "hovering" is a translation of the Hebrew word "*rachaph*", which means to "brood", as when a hen broods over her chicks. Webster's dictionary gives several definitions of the word "brood": a) "To produce as if by incubation." Some translations of the Bible say "the Spirit of God 'incubated' upon the face of the waters." b) "To sit quietly and thoughtfully or to meditate." When a person broods, he ponders something over and over in his mind. That is a form of meditation.

What Genesis 1:2 teaches is that the Spirit of God was meditating the image and vision of God for His creation before He spoke that vision into existence. God thought, He envisioned, He wrote, He meditated and He spoke you, me and this universe into existence. "Therefore be imitators of God as dear children." (Ephesians 5:1) I urge you to grab hold of these truths to create your own world. Your world is your life circumstances - marriage, health, career, finances - everything that pertains to you. You were not created to be a victim, but a victor. You are not God, but you were made by Him to be like Him. He is the CEO, but you have your own branch office. He is the Ruler, but you are His "under-ruler". He is the King of kings. You are one of His "kings". He is the Lord of lords. You are one of His "lords." You have the divine authority and power to take what He has put within you and manifest it in the world.

This should forever put to rest the question whether a steady diet of gangster rap, satanic rock music, profane, violent and pornographic films have an impact on people's behavior. That is not a statistical question; it is a spiritual one. There will never be a satisfactory statistical answer because each person will respond differently. Science deals with measurable results. Spirituality deals with the soul. Some of the results may not be known until eternity. The point here is not to establish scientific fact, but spiritual truth. The argument is not that some teen will listen to violent rap music tonight and go out to commit mass murder tomorrow. Nonetheless, if that youngster continues to "meditate" on those violent, hate filled images and ideas, he or she will be affected in attitude, speech and behavior.

I had a young man tell me about an incident in which gangster rap music had "pumped him up" to find a gun and shoot a boy who had "dissed" – disrespected – him. He said he went home and put on some violent rap music, and the longer he listened the more it seemed right to shoot this other kid. He began to make phone calls to friends, asking if anybody knew where he could get "strapped"," i.e., find a gun. That music became his meditation and it was about to produce two destroyed lives. This was a youngster who often came to church with his family. That, along with some influence from his parents, was the countervailing force which kept his meditation on murder from becoming a tangible reality, but it did affect him. That is undeniable from his own testimony.

No parents would think of allowing their children to feed on a steady diet of physical junk food. No sane person would accept the argument that it will not have an impact on their health and even their behavior as the sugar spikes through their system. Perhaps more important is the awareness that while you may not see results immediately, long term that child is likely to experience the dramatic destructiveness of such behavior. Heart disease, high blood pressure, strokes, even some forms of cancer are aided by eating wrong foods. Diligent parents know this and want to instill the right habits in their children as an investment in a healthy future. Yet these same "responsible" parents will allow their children to feed on a steady diet of spiritual junk food, assuming that it will have no impact on their lives or behavior. This is a testament to our level of spiritual ignorance.

Of course their ignorance is fed and largely caused by the lies in entertainment and media. No company would spend five million dollars to run a thirty second commercial during the Super Bowl if they thought it would have no impact. One Super Bowl commercial by Apple Computer put that company on the minds of millions of people. Yet parents have been sold the lie that an incessant drum beat of violence, sexual perversion and profanity hour after hour, day after day, month after month and year after year will have no impact on our youth or culture. Most people know that fails the test of common sense.

For the last forty years, Americans have had a preoccupation with sexual freedom. It is more accurately described as sexual license and promiscuity. That mindset has produced more children born out of wedlock and raised in divorced or single parent households. It has produced more abortions and an epidemic of teen pregnancy and AIDS. Yet we continue down the same path expecting to somehow solve these social problems while reinforcing the mindset that creates them.

Experiencing a better life on the outside begins with the meditation of a better life on the inside. Changing your life begins with changing your thinking and meditating. The life you have is the life you created. It is up to you to create the life you want.

Don't Worry - Meditate

You were not created to worry. Living a life of worry will destroy you physically, mentally and emotionally. Worry is a form of fear and it will depress and paralyze you if succumb to it. You can practice every principle taught in this book and negate it all by living a life of fear, worry and anxiety. Everything we are talking about here is based upon vital union with the God who loves you in a very personal and intimate way. Worry interferes with that relationship. It indicates that you have more confidence in Satan's ability to do you harm than God's ability to do you good. Fear is not simply the opposite of faith. Fear is faith in an outcome which is contrary to the promises of God. It is lack of confidence in His love, desire and willingness to do you good. It is really faith in Satan's power, which is an insult to God. That is why fear is sin. It is distrust of God. Hebrews 11:6 says, "...without faith it is impossible to please Him..." The scripture also says, "...whatever is not from faith is sin." (Romans 14:23)

Jesus takes a very emphatic stand on worry. He says, "Therefore do not worry, saying, 'What shall we eat?' or 'What shall we drink?' or 'What shall we wear?'... For your Heavenly Father knows that you need all these things." (Matthew 6:31,32) This is a command, not a suggestion. Jesus knows the power of the human being to produce their worst fears. Meditation on the negative will always produce the negative in your life. Meditation on the promises of God to do you good will produce good in your life. He has created in us an unfailing apparatus designed to produce good things in abundance. Jesus says, "But seek first the kingdom of God and His righteousness, and all these things shall be added to you." (Matthew 6:33) This means if you meditate on the abundance of the kingdom of God, all the good things of His Kingdom will come to you. Since "the kingdom of God is within you," (Luke 17:21) the things of the kingdom spring from within you.

If you meditate upon what is terrible, what is frightening, the worst possible scenario, as Job did, the thing you fear and dread will come to you. It will spring forth from within you. You can "worry" yourself into financial failure and bankruptcy, or you can meditate yourself into financial freedom and prosperity. The choice is yours. You can meditate on poverty and lack or you can meditate on the things of the kingdom of God where all things exist in abundance. That abundance is in you already. You are now learning how to tap into it. Isaiah 26:3 says, "You will keep him in perfect peace, whose mind is stayed on You, because He trusts in You." The word peace is the Hebrew word, "shalom" which means "prosperity" -

nothing missing, nothing lacking, nothing broken. If you keep your mind on the problem you will be in perfect poverty –spiritual, mental, emotional and material. If you keep your mind on God, the Problem Solver, you will be kept in or brought into perfect prosperity.

Worry and anxiety are mental habits which are learned. They can be unlearned. You may think worry is a reaction which cannot be helped. That is not true. Worry can be stopped the same way any other bad habit can be stopped. The problem with worry is that unlike other bad habits it infects the core of your life, the inner life, which means that it has devastating impact on your outward life. It is a deadly habit which can and must be defeated.

How does one defeat it? You take control over your emotions by saying something different than what your emotions are telling you. Your emotions are saying, "This is bad! There is no way out! It could not be any worse! You might as well give up! Get a drink! Get some drugs. Find some way to escape the pain!" You can entertain those thoughts, wallow in them and allow them to drag you into depression and despair. Or you can take authority over your emotions. Put a smile on your face. Say out loud "I know God loves me and has the power to help me. I know that He is working in my behalf right now. This situation is going to work out just fine. I do not care how bad things look. I am not moved by what I see. I am not moved by what I feel. I am moved by what I believe, and that is my meditation."

Let your mind, soul and spirit rest in Jeremiah 29:11, which says, "For I know the plans I have for you., declares the Lord, plans to prosper you and not to harm you, plans to give you hope and a future." NIV

Stand on the Word of God and His plan for your life. You will develop a new mental habit. Your mind cannot stay focused on something different than what you are confessing with your mouth. When you start speaking joy with your mouth, your mind will follow and depression will flee. Of course it will try to come back, but stand fast. Make up your mind to drive negative emotions away by replacing them with a new meditation. This will take discipline, practice and persistence, but you can live a worry free life.

You will be amazed at how your decision making, energy and efficiency improve, no longer clouded by the anxiety which once skewed your thinking. It was John, the Apostle of love, who said, "Beloved, I pray that you may prosper in all things and be in health, just as your soul prospers." (3 John 2) Your soul - mind, will and emotions - must prosper in order for you to "prosper and be in health." 1 John 4:18 says, "There is no fear in love; but perfect love casts out fear, because fear involves torment. But he who fears has not been made perfect in love." If you are really perfected or completed by the love of God, you cannot possibly live in fear. God's love - your consciousness of its power and reality - casts it out.

The kind of transforming "agape" love which God offers can only be understood by revelation and received by faith. The Scripture says that the relationship between a man and woman in marriage is akin to the relationship between Christ and the Church. The difference is that

Christ does not divorce, betray or discard His people. Marriage has been turned into a temporary convenience when it was intended to be a life long committed relationship. Modern society no longer adheres to God's design for the institution of marriage. My wife and I were watching television recently as it described the marriage of a famous actress. One friend being interviewed said before the marriage, "You could just see that they were in love. She was just giddy." Less than a year later when they were divorced, another friend said, "They were much better as friends than they were as a married couple." How quickly things change.

God's love is a permanent, unending reality. The rejection of His great love does have certain dire consequences in the end because it necessitates separation from Him. Yet His desire is to love us throughout eternity.

Hollywood sets trends in America and the world. Unfortunately, Hollywood's trends tend to be the wrong ones. Through music, movies, twisted ideas and highly publicized immoral behavior, they create a mass perception which affirms the worst in people. Decades ago the late Whitney Houston had a hit song called "The Greatest Love". The relevant line in the song was, "Learning to love yourself is the greatest love of all." It may be a nice song with a nice tune, but it is wrong. The greatest love of all is not learning to love yourself. The greatest love of all is God's love for you.

The second greatest love is your love for God. Loving yourself is appropriate in light of God's love for you. The second greatest commandment is to love others as you love yourself. That self love must be informed by the love of God. Otherwise, self love becomes megalomania. That is what you hear in rap music – hip hop - today. The songs are all about how talented, big, bad, smart and violent the "rapper" is. That is not the kind of self-love God had in mind when he commanded us to, "love your neighbor as yourself."

It is God's love for you that causes Him to take pleasure in your well being. (Psalm 35:27) You are so precious to Him that He has numbered every hair on your head. (Matthew 10:30) He sent His own Son to be the sacrifice for your sins, that you could be acquitted and worthy to be with Him forever. He loves you so much that He is obsessed with you. He cannot take His eyes off you. He loves you infinitely and perfectly, as if you were the only person on earth. How can you worry and fret in the face of such overpowering love? Remember that God is not an impotent Father who loves His children, but is unable to do anything for them. There is nothing He cannot do. Meditate on the plan, the will, the Word and the love of God, and you will unlock the power of God in your life. When you worry, you block the power.

Seven Keys to Effective Meditation

1. Make your meditation Biblical. Your meditation should be rooted and grounded in the promises of God for your prosperity and abundance.

2. Make your meditation personal. I can give you guidance, but your meditation should be designed to meet the challenges and dreams of your own life, not someone else's.

3. Make your meditation memorable. Keep your meditation simple enough that you can engage in it wherever you are, without referring to notes.

4. Make your meditation continual. Continue meditating that thought or idea until you see the desired results. Do it everyday. Make it part of your regular prayer life.

5. Make your meditation visual. You must see in your "mind's eye" the result you are meditating.

6. Make your meditation visceral. It should be so much a part of you that it arises almost as a spiritual instinct out of the depths of your being.

7. Make your meditation verbal. Silent meditation is soothing and wonderful, but meditation should sometimes include saying out loud the things you are meditating. This will help you stay focused, and there is power in the spoken word.

We began this chapter talking about Joshua. God told him that meditation was to be an ongoing part of his spiritual life and that as a result, Joshua would make his way prosperous and have good success. Would you like to be as successful as Joshua? He caused the Jordan River to be parted miraculously while the people passed over. He led the children of Israel into the promised land. He caused the sun and the moon to stand still while he won a battle against the Amorites (Joshua 10).

Songs are still sung about how Joshua fought the battle of

Jericho and the walls came tumbling down miraculously. The Lord Himself appears to Joshua (Joshua 5). Under Joshua's leadership, God gave the children of Israel peace and rest from all their enemies. (Joshua 23) If these events seem too amazing to believe, consider the God behind the man. The God who slung this vast universe into place is the God who makes the impossible look easy. He will cause the "Jordan River" that stands between you and your "promised land" to part so that you can cross over to the other side. He will cause the sun to stand still in your life so that you can have the light necessary to win the battles of life. He will cause the Jericho walls in your life to fall at your feet miraculously. The Lord of heaven will make Himself known to you and give you prosperity and rest.

7

7TH PRINCIPLE

"Do It"

Everything we have talked about up to now has to do with faith, the heart, the spirit. Each of the principles you have learned can be implemented without making a single telephone call, appointment, investment or anything else on the natural, material plane. This is the axiom by which the universe and all material things were created: FIRST THE SPIRITUAL, THEN THE NATURAL. FIRST THE UNSEEN, THEN THE SEEN.

As a Christian, if you want to affect powerful results in this earthly realm, you must unlock and access the spiritual realm. The spiritually dead person knows only what is earthly and tangible. The scripture describes such people as limited: "But the natural man does not receive the things of the Spirit of God, for they are foolishness to him; nor can he know them because they are spiritually discerned." (1 Corinthians 2:14) They are those "whose end is destruction, whose god is their belly, and whose glory is their shame – who set their mind on earthly things." (Philippians 3:19) The fact that you are reading this book means that you are not one of them and do not want to be.

Let me warn you that there is a "spirituality" that is not of God. There are those who engage in witchcraft, fortune telling, Tarot Card, tea leaf and palm reading and other "spiritual" practices. These practices are wrong and dangerous. They are spoken of as an "abomination" – a particularly detestable sin - in the sight of God. They bring a terrible curse on the person who engages in such things, and you do so at your own peril. The people who engage in such practices have a kind of "faith" of course, but it is the wrong kind of faith in the wrong kind of things. It may produce temporary results, but the forces they unleash are evil and destructive.

The principles that enhance our lives are not a way to win the lottery, succeed at the race track or even gamble in the stock market. They are designed to liberate you from foolish and irresponsible behavior. They will not bring you "good luck" because there is no such thing in God's Kingdom. These principles bring the blessing of God into your life and open you to receive the wonderful things He wants to do for you.

We have come to the point of discussing the tangible action you must take to receive the very best God has. You must do something.

When it is time to take action, that action must be "God-directed" or, to put it another way, "Spirit-led." The question is how to know when and what you are supposed to do? Do I choose this job or that one? Do I invest here or there? Do I marry this person or should I not? Should I start that business now or wait? Should I go after that promotion or wait for a better time? Decisions, decisions.

How do you decide? There are several fundamentals you must keep in mind.

1 - Your Actions Should Line Up With God's Word.

The first principle of decision making for success is enunciated in Romans 8:14, which says, "For as many as are led by the Spirit of God, these are the sons of God." God is never going to lead you in a way inconsistent with His Word. That eliminates many options which you might otherwise consider. God's prosperity cannot involve lying, stealing or cheating. Those actions violate the Word of God.

You are not to be led by your "feelings," for they are subject to change in a moment. Feelings are inherently unreliable as a guide for life. For example, God is not going to have a Christian marry an atheist, agnostic or anyone who is hostile toward God and rejects Jesus Christ. The Bible says, "Do not be unequally yoked together with unbelievers." (2 Corinthians 6:14) We are not supposed to obey our feelings, but the word of God.

God is not going to tell you to take a job involving an illegal or immoral activity. One reason is that those kinds of activities do not produce a prosperous life.

I have seen feelings lead to some absolutely awful decisions in marriage, business and careers. The key to extraordinary life as a Christian is to be led by the Spirit.

He will always lead you toward fulfillment of His Word, even if it doesn't always look or feel like it. God takes pleasure in the prosperity of His servant. (Psalm 35:27) Therefore He will not lead you into poverty. God has said He sent His Word to heal you. (Psalm 107:20) Therefore God will not lead you into any decision or action which results in making you sick. Jesus is the author and finisher of your faith. (Hebrews 12:2) Therefore, He cannot be the author of your failure. Anything that tends toward your detriment is not a decision God is leading you into. Of course I am excluding suffering and even martyrdom for the cause of Christ. I do not consider these detrimental, certainly not in the eternal sense.

Never separate your action from the Word of God. Jesus said, "…[T]ill heaven and earth pass away, one jot or one tittle will by no means pass from the law till all is fulfilled." (Matthew 5:18) The word "jot" is a translation of the Greek letter "iota", which is ancestor of the English letter "i". You have heard the expression "dot the 'i's' and cross the 't's'. God is going to make sure every "i" is dotted and every "t" is crossed. He is absolutely committed to the fulfillment of His Word. God says, "for I am ready to perform My word." Jeremiah 1:12) When your desire is tied to His Word, your desire must be fulfilled. Jesus said, in John 15:7, "If you abide in Me, and My words abide in you, you will ask what you desire, and it shall be done for you."

It is easier for the world to pass away than for you to fail if you are standing on God's word. Let His Word guide you in any important decision of your life.

2 - Know that God is absolutely obligated to make His will clear to you if you ask Him.

He has obligated Himself to those who put their trust in Him. "For if the trumpet makes an uncertain sound, who shall prepare for battle?" (1 Corinthians 14:8) God knows that you cannot be expected to follow directions if those directions are not clear. Are you confused? "...God is not the author of confusion, but of peace...." (1 Corinthians 14:33) The problem that people have with hearing from God is that they have their own pre-dispositions which God has to overcome. He will not violate your will. If you want the benefit of His direction, you must open yourself to it. Neither is God a rubber stamp for your desires. You cannot receive His counsel by first deciding what you want to do and then expecting God to approve it. He does not work that way.

The scripture says, "Trust in the Lord with all your heart, and lean not on your own understanding; in all your ways acknowledge Him and He shall direct your paths." (Proverbs 3:5,6) How are you led by God? You begin by believing that if you acknowledge Him in all your ways, He will direct your paths. That is how you access the power to be led. Do not bog down with questions as to "How?" and "When?" He will do it. Will He speak to me in an audible voice? Not likely. In a dream? In a vision? None of these questions matter. God made no promise as to how He would direct you. He has simply promised that He will. Stand in faith on that promise.

Your own understanding can get in the way. I was

trained as an attorney. My education at Harvard Law School has at times been a hindrance by training me to rely solely on logical analysis to understand any situation. Lawyers of course are trained to think that way, and that is exactly the way I handled my clients' cases and matters before a judge.

However, when it comes to the issues of life, the conscious mind has a very limited perspective. Some problems outstrip human ability. The finest education and the most compelling logic are inadequate in such situations. I am convinced that some insights people have had in critical moments were the blessing of Almighty God. Someone was praying, even if it was not the person who needed the help, but an intercessor. To "lean not" on your own understanding is not to ignore what can be rationally understood. It is merely to recognize the limited nature of that information and to turn to Him who knows everything about everything.

Deeper insight and revelation comes through the spirit rather than through the brain. It will ultimately reach the mind and give you the basis for action, but it will originate in the spirit. God must bypass your thinking apparatus sometimes to say what you may not be ready to grasp with your rational understanding. He may want to take you where you do not expect to go for reasons that you have not yet come to realize. Do not lean on your own understanding because it is too limited.

Many years ago, when my wife and I moved from Massachusetts to Virginia, we had to sell our home. The family who bought it had tried a few months previously to buy another home near ours. After months of effort, they were unable to consummate the deal and lost $10,000. We put our home up for sale on a Sunday. They signed a purchase and sale agreement with us the following Wednesday and purchased it without a hitch. They had always admired the house, but never expected it to become available. God knew that we were going to put it up for sale. Had they not leaned on their own understanding but on God, He would have told them not to try to purchase that first house, but to wait. He might have even told them that our house, the one they really wanted, was soon to become available. Their human intellect could not have known any of this, but God did. They wasted $10,000 plus time and energy.

An evangelist was about to purchase a building. God revealed to him that a certain church building, which at the time was not for sale, was to be the sight of his new school. Unbeknownst to him, that Pastor was putting that building up for sale. The evangelist bought that building. Had he not been listening to God, he might have hired a realtor and purchased the wrong property. He avoided what could have been a disaster by leaning not to his own understanding.

My wife and I moved to Virginia because we became convinced that God wanted us there. We planned to put our Massachusetts house up for sale in the spring, have it sold by middle to late summer and move in late August or early September. Our house sold so fast that we ended up buying our new home in April, right after our Massachusetts house went under contract to the buyers. We planned to come to Virginia in April just to "look".

Instead we had to buy quickly because our old house was sold before we expected.

We had another timing problem. When we found the builder we liked, he informed us it would take five months to construct our house. We would be out of our old house in the middle of July, but our new house would not be ready until late September to early October. This was unworkable. Then the builder remembered that there was a home already under construction - the very model we liked. It would be ready at just the right time. On the other hand, it was still early enough in construction that my wife could make changes in the architectural plans with no added cost. The timing turned out to be perfect. After closing on the sale of our old home, we spent one night in a hotel in Boston and one night in a hotel in Virginia before moving into the new house. It worked out that way because we were being obedient to God, not leaning to our own understanding. The same can happen for you.

The second prerequisite to hearing from God is that you must have patience. You must be willing to wait for directions from Him. You cannot simply jump precipitously because you feel like it or you do not want to wait. There is a time for action, but you must make sure that it is the right time. God knows your timing needs. Remember that He has all aspects of a situation in mind at once. You have a very limited perspective.

The third prerequisite to hearing from God is to be seeking righteousness and holiness. I am not talking about perfection. You will never be perfect here on earth, but you do not have to wallow in sin either. We are living in a world where feelings take precedence over facts. Emotions are powerful, but that doesn't make them an accurate moral barometer. Being "in love" does not make sex outside marriage right. Same sex attraction doesn't make homosexuality right. Feeling that your biological and genetic gender is not who you really are does not by definition prove that changing your identity is the moral thing to do. What makes human beings moral creatures is that we have the ability to make choices in direct opposition to how we feel. A man or woman may feel a powerful emotional and sexual attraction to someone other than the spouse. They can also choose to do what is morally right by ignoring those feelings and being faithful to the covenant of marriage.

In other words, if you want God's guidance, you must commit to taking the moral high ground. You cannot lie, steal, cheat and con your way through life, and yet expect God's guidance when you decide you need it.

I must confess to you that I considered leaving out of this book any mention of sin. Our world, including my own country - the United States - is embracing the idea that there is no such thing as sin. Many, particularly in media and entertainment believe that the concept of sin is judgmental. They're right. It is. The judgment is not mine but God's. Those who condemn others for acknowledging this truth do not have an argument with me, but with God and the Bible.

I am also keenly aware as someone who is deeply involved in the politics of our country, that this may come back to haunt me because the mainstream media has a peculiar aversion to Bible believing Christians. I do not believe it is overstating the case to say that they really hate us, but I would love to be proved wrong. It would be easier for me to avoid the hard truth. However, this is not a political treatise on foreign or domestic policy. This is a personal book written to individual Christians who want to do better in life. I am telling you without apology that sin will get in the way, and you will have to pay for it sooner or later. If you want the best in life, stay away from it. While I realize it is a bit cliche, it still bears repeating that the Decalogue which God gave Moses was not ten suggestions, but Ten Commandments.

What if you have sinned or are now living a sinful lifestyle? Repent. Ask God to forgive you, cleanse you and deliver you. He will. You cannot receive God's best when you are burdened with sin. Only the blood of Jesus can bring you the deliverance and forgiveness you need.

The fourth prerequisite is to be committed in advance to obeying what He tells you to do. It will not work to say, ""Lord, once I hear what you have to say, I'll then decide whether to obey."

After I graduated from law school, I wanted to return to Philadelphia, near where I grew up in Chester, Pennsylvania. I thought I consulted God about it, but in fact, I merely assumed that because that was what I wanted to do, it was what God wanted me to do. I could not have been more wrong. I searched and searched for the right job in a law firm in Philadelphia. Nothing developed. The firms I wanted did not want me. The ones which wanted me I did not want.

By the late spring of my year of graduation, I began to worry. I did not know at that stage of my spiritual life how not to worry. However, since I was a Christian by that time, I also began to pray earnestly for direction. One one occasion I prayed all night long. After a lot of frustration, I finally surrendered. I let God know for the first time that I would go wherever He wanted me to go. The day after making that commitment, I received a call from a Boston firm offering me a job . I knew then that I was to stay in Boston.

Up until that time, I had been saying that if necessary I would move to the Philadelphia area without a job and stay with my father until I found the right job. That would have been a very stupid and rebellious thing to do. I thought I was showing determination, but in actuality it was stubbornness. I had not asked God what he wanted for me. I was too busy seeking my own will. Boston proved to be precisely where I belonged at that stage of my life. My wife and I successfully raised our children and made a contribution there. I established Boston's first and only gospel radio station.

Boston was the place where God matured my character and taught me how to walk by faith and follow Him. When you follow Him, you will never fail.

God wants to lead and guide you to a great destiny. He desperately wants you to follow Him so that you can experience the best He has for you. This is not to say there will be no trials. Jesus said, "In the world You shall have tribulation..." He did not say you might, but that you will. Yet He also promised that you would overcome the world with your faith.

It is not necessary that you be consciously aware that God is directing you in a specific situation. It may be that you are taking the next logically indicated or responsible thing to do. It may be in hindsight that you realize that you were being directed by God. What you must do is submit the matters of life to Him and believe that He will do what is necessary to direct your action and decisions.

The Book of Esther is a wonderful example of this. Haddasah is a Jewish woman living in Exile in Persia. By the providence of God she becomes Queen. Esther was her Persian name. After she took office however, a crisis developed. A wicked member of the King's court - Haman - conspired to kill all the Jews. He did not know that Esther was a Jew. Her uncle made her aware of the situation, telling her in effect that God made her Queen to save the Jews from Haman's plan for their destruction. For the first time, she became aware that God had been guiding her all along. She then had to decide whether she would be obedient to Him or look out for herself. She made the right decision, and saved the lives of the Jewish people in Persia, destroying wicked Haman at the same time. You need not be conscious of God's specific leading, but when you become aware, you have a responsibility to submit.

Anyone who knows and serves Jesus Christ will acknowledge in hindsight that we were "led" in certain ways by God before we came to Him. God knew that we were to become His and protected us from self-destruction. Most of us were oblivious to that truth. I certainly was. He led me nevertheless. "For whom He foreknew, He also predestined to be conformed to the image of His Son... Moreover whom He predestined, these He also called, whom He called, these He also justified, and whom He justified, these He also glorified." (Romans 8:29,30) God knows who will respond to His call and who will not, and He gently protects His own until they consciously decide to submit to Him.

This process continues to some extent after a person has made a conscious decision to submit to God's leadership. I spoke earlier about moving South. I knew seven years before that move that we would be leaving Boston, but I did not know where God would send us. In 1996 I went to a meeting in Houston, which lead to a project which brought me to Virginia from time to time. It was during one of those trips that I realized we were moving to Virginia. The process which led to the move had begun seven years earlier. Little did I know that my trip to Houston in 1996 was the first stop in discovering our new home in Virginia. I only realized that in hindsight.

The story of Joseph, beginning in chapter 37 of the Book of Genesis, is another example of the leading of God when people are unaware that it is happening. God protected Joseph from his jealous brothers desire to kill him. God's purpose was to get Joseph into Egypt and raise him to the highest seat of government under Pharaoh. He became a man of immense wealth and prosperity. When the famine came, Joseph was in control of the food supply.

Understand that God did not engineer the jealousy of Joseph's brothers, nor the other terrible things that happened to him. Sometimes however, within the framework of God's purposes, He uses the evil men do to accomplish His own ends. Joseph's testimony to his brothers when they were finally reunited was, "...[Y] ou meant evil against me; but God meant it for good, in order to bring it about as it is this day, to save many people alive." (Genesis 50:20) Joseph only knew this in hindsight, but through every twist and turn of his life, he continued to trust God.

We learn two important lessons from these stories. First, the plan of God always takes into account the sinfulness of human beings. He is not the author of their evil, but the One who brings out of that evil something redemptive. God does not will anyone to do evil, but He will not violate the freedom He has given mankind, even when that freedom is used to do evil.

The second lesson is that God's plan is always working out the adversity of life for your good. He is constantly turning curses into blessings to demonstrate His goodness. There was great adversity in the lives of Esther, Joseph and a host of others, including you. Yet God turns that adversity into something good.

When you find yourself in a situation where you did not plan to be, remember that God is able to do the "exceeding abundantly above what we ask or think." (Ephesians 3:20) He is leading you into something far better than you can plan or achieve by your own effort alone.

Of course as you mature in your faith walk, you will often be conscious that God is leading you. Here are some keys to consciousness that God is directing you. First seek direction from Him. Do not make any significant decision in life without consulting Him. If you are hesitant about consulting God, you probably do not want to hear what you suspect God will say. He may tell you that is the wrong man or woman to marry. He may tell you that is the wrong job. Ignoring His direction only puts you in peril.

As a child I admired Cadillac automobiles. I set a goal for myself to have a Cadillac by the age of thirty. I decided to beat my own deadline and get my first Cadillac at the age of about 28. There was just one problem. I did not have the money. Somehow, I thought, "If I buy it, the money will come." Wrong! I bought it. Not only was this white, Eldorado Cadillac beyond my income, but it was the worst car I ever bought. I had misgivings about buying it, but I took the position that because I wanted it so much, God surely wanted me to have it. Wrong again!

That car turned out to be an albatross around my neck. It had a diesel engine which was hard to start in a cold Boston winter. To add insult to injury, the heater never worked properly. Imagine riding in one of the most stylish vehicles anyone could own with the temperature inside the car at 25 degrees. I looked great, but my teeth were chattering. I spent more time in the repair shop than on the road. Something was always going wrong with that car. I had to get rid of it after only six months, and was forced to sue the dealer to be released from the debt. It was a curse from day one. I am convinced that if I had prayed and sincerely consulted with God, I would never have bought it.

I learned my lesson. Every car I've owned since then

has been a blessing. In fact I cannot remember when I was last in an automobile accident. It has been well over twenty-five years.

There is a seeking and knocking process in taking the appropriate action. In Matthew 7:7-8, Jesus gave a spiritual formula. He said, "Ask, and it will be given to you; seek, and you will find; knock and it will be opened to you. For everyone who asks receives, and he who seeks finds, and to him who knocks it will be opened." Notice that there are three steps involved. The asking is prayer. We have already discussed that in great detail. The "seeking" refers to the action necessary to "find" what you are asking for. The "knocking" involves locating the correct door to what you have requested. Every material thing God is going to give you will come through some earthly means. The source is heavenly, but the means will be earthly. Once you have begun to pray, believe, envision, speak, write and meditate, you must seek the avenue through which your desire will come. If you are looking for a car, you might search online or visit car dealers and tell others what kind of car you want. When you think you have found what you are seeking, you knock on that door to see if it opens for you. If you fail to take the appropriate action, what is waiting for you will sit there unclaimed, just like a package left at the post office and never picked up.

Sometimes a door will appear locked until you try it. When my wife and I know people are coming to visit our home, we often unlock the door. When guests arrive, they usually assume the door is locked. If I am sitting where they can see me, I wave them in. They turn the knob and realize that the door is open, not locked. Following God's direction can be like that. He has always opened the door in advance, but it may appear locked. You knock and God will wave you in.

The second step in this process is to listen for instruction. God does not show you His whole plan at once. He paves the way as you go. Walking by faith means that you do not need to see how everything will work. Your task is to be obedient as He leads you step by step. One of the greatest miracles of scripture was the parting of the Red Sea which allowed the children of Israel to cross safely to the other side. Consider that the escaping slaves did not know that the Red Sea was going to part. God told Moses to lead them forward. The Sea parted as they obeyed.

Do not expect God to speak to you in an audible voice. God usually speaks to us by creating a deep and abiding sense of conviction. When it happens, you know it. If you are receptive, He will make sure that you know what you need to know. There are people who think that they can make decisions without direction from God because they are intelligent or well educated. I have made that mistake and it can be disastrous.

Once you are clear that you have heard from God, take the step of faith. Do what God has instructed you to do, even if it doesn't seem to make sense. The Pastor of a local church was in a building program, but it had stalled. He had raised only $10,000 – far less than needed to relocate to a new building. After seeking direction from God, he received instructions. He was to take that $10,000 and give it to a ministry which was also in a building program, but farther along in the process, accomplishing what he had not yet managed. This seems crazy in the eyes of most people, but that Pastor put into operation a spiritual law. That law produced the ideal building for his church within a few short months after taking God-directed action.

The fourth thing you should do in hearing and obeying God's direction is to look for the open door. Jesus says, "See, I have set before you an open door, and no one can shut it..." (Revelation 3:8) The door that God has opened for you cannot be shut by anyone. No one can walk through the door that God has prepared for you unless you refuse it. The door that is for you, He "shuts [to others] and no one opens." (Revelation 3:7) A corollary of this principle is to beware the closed door. If you must beat your head bloody trying to break through a door, it is probably not for you. Satan will place obstacles in your path especially when you are on the path God has for you. You must learn to discern the difference between obstacles placed by the enemy and simply being on the wrong path. Generally, when the enemy is trying to obstruct you, the problems will disappear as you attack them spiritually. When you are on the wrong path, the problems and obstacles will be intractable and tend to intensify instead of receding.

There is one further very important distinction to be made as you launch into decision making and action. The choice you must make is not always one between good and evil or best and worst. The choice will sometimes be between good, better and best. God always wants the best for you. In God's economy, "good enough" is not good enough. Only the best is good enough for God. He wants to teach us to "approve the things that are excellent."

(Philippians 1:10) Here again, you may not be able to fathom with human reasoning what is truly "best" because it may not become apparent until farther down the road.

For example, you have two job offers. Both look very good. Both companies are solid, pay well and offer upward mobility. Assuming that all things are basically equal, which do you choose? What you do not know is that on one job you will end up working for a senior officer with whom you have good chemistry. You will be promoted quickly and end up running the company sooner than anyone could have imagined. In the other job, you will be laid off within six months because the company will face an unexpected financial crisis. Both look good on the surface, but one has unexpected problems that only God can see. By the way, God may indeed lead you to the job that will soon face problems, but it will be because it is the key to something better He has in store for you. You need Divine wisdom and insight to know what to do in these situations. God wants you to experience the highest and best, but He sees that clearly and you do not. Trust him.

Pay close attention to inner uneasiness as you contemplate important choices. That sense of uneasiness may be wisdom coming deep from within you which you ignore to your detriment. One of the greatest mistakes of my ministry was to ignore that inner restraint, charging ahead to make an important appointment to a ministry assignment. The cost was devastating. God was speaking to me, but I ignored His inner voice, and listened to "logic". Six months later, my logic proved disastrous. You may not be able to articulate that sense of uneasiness or why it is there, but do not deny it a place in your thinking. It may save you a great deal of heartache.

The scripture says God's Word is "a lamp to my feet and a light to my path." (Psalm 119:105) That means that the Word of God illuminates the road so that you can see more clearly. When you are driving your car at night down a dark, unfamiliar road, you turn on the "bright lights." Then you can see farther. Things which were shadowy now come to the light. You can navigate that curve or exit ramp ahead. The Word of God is like a bright light that will shine on the path of your life, allowing you to navigate the journey to your destiny.

Dreams and Visions

We all dream, but few understand the power of dreams and visions to give supernatural guidance or confirmation. The scripture says, "For God may speak in one way or in another, yet man does not perceive it. In a dream, in a vision of the night, when deep sleep falls upon men, while slumbering on their beds, then He opens the ears of men and seals their instruction." (Job 33:14-16) This text points out that when God does speak, often we are not receptive enough to hear Him. Therefore, it is necessary at times for God to bypass the conscious and go directly to the unconscious through a dream. Keep in mind of course that most dreams are not a message from God. Some dreams are no more than a message from the pizza you ate or the bad movie you watched the night before.

What is the difference between the dream that is a

message and the dream that should be ignored? First, God does not speak in nightmares. He does not create fear. "...[P]erfect love casts out fear..." (1 John 4:18) Your nightmares are the work of the evil imaginations you have invited into your mind and the wicked spiritual forces which seek to invade your life. The best way to deal with them is to reject their messages along with the fear they inspire. Put your trust in God, and the nightmares will leave you.

Second, the dreams that come from God are vivid. You will remember details as if you were watching a movie. Many times we barely remember what we have dreamed. When God gives you direction through a dream, the dream will be clear. You will know that your dream is something more than the usual. It will make an impression. It may take time, prayer and patience to get the proper interpretation. Sometimes God gives you a dream to confirm something that is yet to come so that when it comes you will know that God has already confirmed it. When you arrive at the moment of fulfillment, you will know that this is God.

Before we purchased our present home, I had a dream about the house in which we then lived. I saw trees growing right through the floor. Not just one or two, but many trees. They were large and tall. In the dream I was alarmed, thinking, "This is terrible". God spoke to me in the dream with the thought that this was a sign of great prosperity. I took it as such and filed it away in my heart. When months later we purchased our new home, that dream came back to me. As I was driving into the development one day, I remembered that it was built in what had been a forest of tall trees. Many were left standing to beautify the development. What I had seen in my dream was the location of our future home, a home built where many large, tall trees once stood. That was a confirming dream to let me know that I was in the right place. I did not realize that until I got there. Relocating seven hundred miles from one state to another was not easy. It was comforting to have confirmation that I made the right decision. Of course God communicated His approval in a variety of ways. That was one of them. He will do the same for you if you are open to hearing Him.

I am not telling you to govern your life or make decisions on the basis of dreams. It is simply one of the myriad ways God will give you guidance and direction. Before you act on any dream, make very sure that it is consistent with the Word of God and in keeping with other signals that you are getting from God. I did not move my family based on a dream. That was the result of years of prayer, listening to God and discussion with my wife. The dream was an after-the-fact confirmation, not the basis for my decision. The most important thing to remember is to be sincere about listening to and obeying God.

8

8TH PRINCIPLE

"Give It"

J esus said, "It is more blessed to give than to receive."." The key to experiencing the greatest blessings of God is to be "a blessing." God told Abraham, "I will bless you...and you shall be a blessing...And in you all the families of the earth shall be blessed." (Genesis 12:2,3) God's purpose is to reach the world. Anyone who desires to be blessed by God must also desire to be a blessing.

God hears a never ending list of requests for help and resources. What He lacks are people willing to be the answer for others, to be the resource others need. Too few willing to be the mechanism He uses to bless others. Psalm 112 describes the person who becomes God's vessel of distribution. "Wealth and riches will be in his house... He has dispersed abroad, He has given to the poor; his righteousness endures forever." (Psalm 112:3,9) Notice carefully the tenses in the Psalm. The wealth and riches "will" be in his house. Before that happens however, he "has" dispersed abroad and given to the poor. Giving is not something you do after you prosper. It is a life long practice which causes you to prosper.

Making a commitment to give triggers the spiritual law of sowing and reaping. "[W[hatever a man sows, that he will also reap." (Galatians 6:7) This is an absolute law, more certain than gravity. Jesus rose to heaven in a cloud, defying earth's gravity. (Acts 1:9,10) He appeared and disappeared at will, obviously traveling from one place to another without being subject to the "time" it takes to get there. He also went through walls, entering rooms without coming through the door and thereby defying natural limitations of space. (Luke 24:31; John 20:26) Spiritual law transcends natural laws. Spiritual laws are absolute truth, not relative or dependent on time and place. They never change.

The law of sowing and reaping says whatever you give, will come back to you for good or for ill. If you give hatred, you will receive hatred. Give love, and you will receive love. Give money, and you will receive money. Show interest in others, and others will show interest in you. Whatever you sow or put out will be come back to you.

The Bible says, "Give and it shall be given to you; good measure, pressed down, shaken together, and running over will be put into your bosom. For with the same measure that you use, it will be measured back to you." (Luke 6:38) This aspect of the law provides that you will not only receive in kind, but also in quantity based on your giving. Do you want to receive more? Give more. If your giving is in generous portions, you will receive in generous portions. "He who sows sparingly will also reap sparingly, and he who sows bountifully will also reap bountifully." (2 Corinthians 9:6) If you lack money, give it. If you do not have any money to give, give something else of value. You need to make the quality decision to be a giver.

There is no virtue in poverty. Poor people can be just as stingy, mean and selfish as people with money. Money is not the root of all evil. The Bible says, "For the love of money is the root of all kinds of evil." (1 Timothy 6:10) Money is not evil, nor does it make people evil. Money does not change a person's character, but magnifies who people really are. God is the creator of silver and gold. There was gold in the Garden of Eden, and God said that the gold was good. (Genesis 2:12) God says, "The silver is Mine, and the gold is Mine..." (Haggai 2:8) There is also gold in heaven. It is of such a pure nature that it is as clear as glass. That is God's gold. (Revelation 21:18,21) If it were evil, God would never associate Himself with it. God doesn't want us to love or trust money, but He also knows that in this world we need it.

There are many stories in the Bible which have been misinterpreted to imply that money in and of itself is bad. One such story is that of the rich young ruler. He had obeyed the basic commandments, and thought he wanted to follow Christ. Jesus said to him, "You still lack one thing. Sell all that you have and distribute to the poor, and you will have treasure in heaven; and come and follow Me." (Luke 18:22)

The Apostles had been successful businessmen in the fishing industry. After the incident with the young ruler, Jesus told them it is very difficult for a rich man to enter the kingdom of heaven. Their response was not that of poor men. They said, "Who then can be saved?" If they had been poor, their response would have been, "Those rich people are in big trouble." They obviously saw themselves as rich. Matthew had been a tax collector. There was no such thing as a poor tax collector. Tax collectors were despised, but they had money. That is partly why they were so disliked. Yet God chose a tax collector.

God was not trying to get the rich young ruler to be poor as if poverty itself was something to be desired. He was trying to get him to transfer his trust from money to God. God does not want you to be poor. He wants you to have more than enough, but He wants to be your source. "And God is able to make all grace abound toward you, that you, always having all sufficiency in all things, may have an abundance for every good work." (2 Corinthians 9:8)

"Do not lay up for yourselves treasures on earth where moth and rust destroy and where thieves break in and steal; but lay up for yourselves treasures in heaven, where neither moth nor rust destroys and where thieves do not break in and steal. For where your treasure is there will your heart be also." (Matthew 6:19-21)

This text teaches us to place our treasures in God's care. When He is the caretaker of your wealth, it will not rust away and no thief can steal it. When you give into God's kingdom - to churches, ministries and nonprofits dedicated to advancing the gospel - you cannot lose your investment. It is forever recorded in heaven, and you will get a return, with eternal interest.

Tithing

A great deal has been written and said about tithing.

It is the only form of giving for which God issues a challenge to test His promise. "Bring all the tithes into the storehouse, that there may be food in My house, and try Me now in this," says the Lord of hosts, "if I will not open for you the windows of heaven and pour out for you such blessing that there will not be room enough to receive it." (Malachi 3:10) What God is saying is that if you are in Covenant with Him, you may test His faithfulness by tithing.

This offer is so astounding that those who think that we do not have to tithe "today" are missing a great opportunity. God is offering to display His power to prosper those who are faithful to Him.

God does not promise to pour out "blessings" – plural, but rather a "blessing" – singular. The blessing is an empowerment to prosper. It is so great that there is no room to receive it. Your imagination needs to be stretched to fully comprehend how abundantly God wants to prosper you.

It is the same principle reflected in Ephesians 3:20, "exceedingly abundantly above all that we ask or think, according to the power that works in us." The power that "works in us" is "the blessing", the empowerment to create. This is intended only for those who are in Covenant relationship with God through Jesus Christ. Tithing gives you access to what God wants you to have.

If you want to experience the best life has to offer, give. Make giving your lifestyle. Bless your family. Help others. Win others to Jesus Christ by your generosity, testimony and love. Glorify God in giving and watch Him shower you with more.

9

9TH PRINCIPLE

"Receive It"

For some people this commandment is more difficult than the commandment to give. Human pride, religious tradition and a false sense of independence make it difficult for some to be receivers. There is very little emphasis given to the role of receiving in creating prosperity, yet the importance of receiving cannot be overestimated.

As has already been mentioned, God is not going to rain down hundred dollar bills from heaven. Whatever He wants to get into your hands is going to come through a human vessel. Therefore, being willing to receive from God, means being willing to receive from others. Jesus said, "Give and it shall be given to you..." You must give, but you must also receive. You should continue casting bread on the water, but you must also accept it when it comes back to you. Just as God blesses you for giving to others, you must allow Him to bless others for giving to you. Just as you give in faith, receive in faith.

As a pastor, I want the best for my flock. I want to see them healthy and successful in their careers. I want them to have strong marriages, bright, healthy children who love their parents and love God. It would be the height of foolishness to say that I have no interest in their financial prosperity. Of course I want them to have more than enough money. I want the same for you, and so does God. Think about it. Do you want your children to live in poverty?

A minister who truly believes that giving is a key to prosperity will never refuse to receive anything from a person who gives with sincerity of heart. I will not receive a gift from someone who I know is using it to manipulate me or to accomplish some hidden agenda. If a person wants to give his last dollar with a pure heart, I will receive it. That dollar will do him little good if he keeps it. Neither is it enough to do me any good financially. However, it will do him a world of good if he sows it in faith. I would be doing him a disservice if I did not receive it. A person who does not believe that will think it criminal to receive a person's last dollar. He would not receive, but neither would he give his last dollar. It makes no sense to the carnal mind. I have given my last because what I had was not enough. I multiplied it by giving it. Someone had to receive my giving. If everyone were too proud to receive, there would be no one to whom we could give.

Many do not understand that this is a prerequisite to the prosperity of God having full sway in your life. God is "able" to give you all you need and desire according to His will, but you have to "receive" it. Jesus has already paid the price for your sins, but you will not be saved until and unless you receive that free gift. God wants to prosper you and He is able to prosper you, but you must receive that prosperity. Jude 24 says He is "able to keep you from stumbling. And to present you faultless before the presence of His glory with exceeding joy..." To be "able" to do something is not saying that it automatically happens. I may be able to give you $10,000, but that does not mean that you will get it. You have to believe and commit to receiving from God just as passionately as you commit to giving to God.

God's ability does not kick in until you commit. We pray over the food we buy, acknowledging that God gave us the food. However, we do not pray over and acknowledge that God gave us the money to buy the food. The reason why people have a hard time receiving is that they receive for themselves rather than receiving for God. Once you "commit" your money to Him, it changes the whole basis and focus for receiving. Until you do this you are trying to handle the matter yourself with human strength instead of His power.

It is after exhortation to give bountifully that the scripture says, "And God is able to make all grace abound toward you that you, always having all sufficiency in all things may have an abundance for every good work." (2 Corinthians 9:8) Of course God wants you to live well. You are His child. Nonetheless, the ultimate purpose of God's financial empowerment in your life is that you have abundance for "every good work." There are good works God wants done. He wants those works done through you. God has plenty of people who need, but fewer who will be used by Him to supply those needs. Become a receiver that you may be a distributor for God. Once you commit to being His giver, abundance is coming back for you to share with others.

God is able to do the "exceedingly abundantly above all that we ask or think" (Ephesians 3:20) but there is a proviso. It is "according to the power that works in us." The word "power" is a translation of the Greek word "dunamis". That is the word from which we derive our English word "dynamite." It is the explosive power of God. That power is placed within us when we surrender ourselves to God, but the power is ignited in particular areas of life only when we commit that area to Him. Human beings have a tendency to compartmentalize our lives into neat little sections. Church is over here. Career is over there. Relationships in another corner. Our physical health is at the gym. Money is another dimension of our lives.

In fact all these areas are deeply spiritual. When we come to realize that we are spiritual beings having a natural experience, instead of thinking of ourselves as physical beings having occasional spiritual experiences, our lives will change dramatically. Affluence requires spiritual wisdom because money is deceitful and subject to abuse. Never use people to get money. Use money to serve and bless people.

As a spiritual experiment I once gave out $20 bills during a worship service. People at first began to squirm in their seats. They had never experienced going to church and being given money. The only financial experience they ever had in Church was giving money. When I turned that paradigm around, they felt uncomfortable. Part of the lesson was that God wants to bless us in unexpected ways. Your job is not the limit of your prosperity. If you think that it is, you have placed a limit on God. He is "able" to help, but not if we refuse to receive. When we refuse to receive from God, our only option is to work more hours, take a second job or borrow more money, none of which leads to financial security or abundance.

This is not to say there is anything inherently wrong with taking a second job or working more hours. I worked two jobs to help pay my way through college. However, that was a temporary sacrifice to achieve a specific goal, not a way to get rich. If you do that as a way of life rather than the means to a particular goal, you will only end up frustrated and probably broke. Giving and receiving should be your way of life as a Christian, and your key to prosperity.

On one occasion I was led to sow into the life of a young man outside of church. He responded by saying, "No I don't take money from people." Now I was not a stranger to him, where he might have a reason to suspect my motives. I did not press the point because I knew that I would get credit for obedience whether he received it or not. Just a few days later, someone came up to me, not knowing what I tried to do for the young man, and put into my hands the exact amount of money that I tried to give away.

If the young man had any spiritual understanding, he would have received that money as a gift from God and turned around and blessed someone else. He would have gotten into the flow of God's economy. When I give I do so in the name of Jesus Christ. I receive in the same way. It is from God, and my first consideration is what God wants me to do with that money. You should give in faith so that the word and power of God will work in your behalf. You receive in faith that your receiving blesses the person you receive from and is an opportunity for you to bless someone else.

When I received the money referred to above, I did not spend a dime of it. I gave it away. I was simply the conduit whereby God moved that money from one individual to another. There are times of course when God gives to me and that money is spent mainly on me or my family, but I am committed at the receiving end to doing whatever God wants me to do with the money that I receive.

Jesus said, "It is more blessed to give than to receive." (Acts 20:35) He does not say that one should not receive. He is saying that giving is the more empowering side of the transaction. The way to bring the two together is that you always receive with a view to giving. However, you do not wait until you have received before you give. Start giving now. The receiving will come.

An acquaintance of mine once told me that he had misgivings about people putting diamond rings and gold watches in the Church offering plate. His attitude began to change when I told him that I would receive such offerings without hesitation, but my first question would be, "God, what do you want me to do with this? I know you have a purpose for delivering this into the ministry. Show me what your purpose is, and I will carry it out." A dear sister donated a fur coat worth about $6,000 into our ministry. I received that fur coat, and blessed her for it. As you will see, had I refused to do so, I would have deprived her and the ministry of tremendous blessings. After praying and thinking about it for a few weeks, I was led to sow it into another ministry. I did so. In less than a year, she was completely out of debt, had a beautiful vehicle paid for, and had given $5,000 cash to the church. The skeptic will call it a coincidence, but I have experienced too many such coincidences to entertain that kind of thinking. These are not coincidences, but God's law in operation. You do not heat a pot of water and call it an interesting "coincidence" when it boils. That is a natural law at work, which will work every time. Giving and receiving works every time.

The other important aspect of receiving is that when you receive, you should bless and pray for the person who gives. When I receive from someone, I pray for them to prosper, to be healed, to have a strong marriage or whatever they may need or desire. When you do that, you are also giving even as you receive.

One other aspect of receiving should be mentioned. There are times when God will bless you through people who have no intention or desire to bless you. In one situation I counseled a woman who was not receiving support from the father of her children and did not know where he was. After sowing a financial gift into the ministry, she suddenly began to receive checks from a government garnishment of his wages. He resisted fulfilling his financial obligations as a father, but she went to God. Let this be a reminder not to limit how God may bless you. You can never anticipate the myriad ways He has of meeting your needs. Just be ready to receive.

The Bible story about Elijah and the widow woman has another instructive aspect to it. When Elijah asked the woman to share what little she had with him, she responded, "...I am gathering a couple of sticks that I may go and prepare it for myself and my son, that we may eat it and die." (1 Kings 17:12) God had told Elijah that He "commanded" this widow woman to feed him. She did not seem to be aware of that. The point is that God has prepared people in advance to help you, whether they know it or not.

Notice that God used someone who had almost nothing. Recall our discussion about receiving the last of what someone has. Had Elijah decided that he could not in good conscience receive from this poor widow, he would have deprived her, her son, and himself of the blessing necessary to keep them all alive.

Beware of criticizing a sincere minister of the gospel for receiving an offering from people who you think cannot "afford" it. What you think they cannot afford may be the key to saving their lives. Those who are impoverished financially cannot afford not to give. Nor can they afford to have the person to whom they are trying to give refuse to receive. One minister told the story of a cleaning woman who earned only a small amount per week. He said that receiving her tithe was difficult. A part of him wanted to refuse it because the woman had so little. Nevertheless, in keeping with the example of Elijah, he received it by faith. The woman had a mentally deficient daughter whom she also taught to tithe. As a result of the blessing she and her mother received through tithing, she overcame her mental deficiency and became a major developer and the wealthiest woman in her town. If that minister had refused that tithe, he might have robbed that woman and her daughter of the blessing of giving to a man of God."

You have the potential to be an extraordinary giver. You must add receiving to the transaction to make it all work for you. I am sowing the information in this book into your life. Receive it. The hours spent writing it are for you. The years spent praying, meditating and thinking about this subject were for you if you will receive them.

Let me give a more personal testimony about what these principles have done for me. When my wife and I were about to relocate from Massachusetts to Virginia, the biggest challenge was financing the move. In order to move and set up an office in Virginia I estimated that I would need $100,000. None of that could come out of the equity in our home, which would be used to purchase our new home. I did not have that kind of money and did not know where I was going to get it. I prayed, meditated and believed God's word. Only one month before I was scheduled to move, a man who had been a modest supporter contacted me. He was interested in what I was doing. We agreed to have dinner. After the meeting, he committed the sum of $100,000 to my work.

When all was said and done he contributed close to $200,000 in the course of a little more than a year. I received it, and through his seed was able to bless many more people. That is the "exceedingly abundantly" we have talked about. Mind you that I did not wait until the day before I was scheduled to move to begin praying and believing. In fact, I had been doing that for years. The house we purchased was my vision long before we moved into it.

Someone who is trying to get out of debt may want to help you pay off a debt. Receive it, and bless them. Someone who wants a new car may help you buy one. Receive it, and bless them. Someone who wants to pay for a child's education may help you pay your child's tuition. Receive it, and bless them. Do not short circuit their blessing or yours. This is not a license to beg for money. These are not principles of manipulation. You do not have to con your way into anything God wants you to have. You do not have to stab others in the back to be blessed. In fact that will lead to the opposite result.

God does not bless people who hurt others to get what they want. Some people cannot be trusted because they are so greedy for money that they will betray anyone to get it. Stay away from those people, and never allow yourself to become one of them.

❝As you have therefore received Christ Jesus the Lord, so walk in Him, rooted and built up in Him and established in the faith, as you have been taught, abounding in it with thanksgiving." (Colossians 2:6,7) When God brings good things into your life, thank Him for it. In fact you should live with an attitude of thanksgiving, always expecting to receive from God and thanking Him in advance. Thanksgiving causes overflow of every good thing in life. Be thankful for where you are right now, and what you have right now. That does not mean to have a lazy satisfaction. It is perfectly appropriate to want more out of life, but you should always be thankful for what you already have. Giving is a great way to express thanks to God for your blessings.

Finally, be a purposeful giver. Whatever I receive has one overriding purpose: to advance the kingdom of God. My first thought is, "How can this be used to advance God's kingdom?" That should be your preoccupation in receiving. How can I advance God's plan, program, love, salvation and every good thing he has in mind for people?

Jesus dealt with this issue when some of His disciples, mainly Judas Iscariot, criticized His receiving. "And when Jesus was in Bethany at the house of Simon the leper. A woman came to him having an alabaster flask of very costly fragrant oil, and she poured it on His head as He sat at table. But when His disciples saw it, they were indignant, saying, 'Why this waste? For this fragrant oil might have been sold for much and given to the poor.' But when Jesus was aware of it, He said to them, 'Why do you trouble the woman? For she has done a good work for Me.'" (Matthew 26:6-10) That spirit of jealousy is alive and well in people today. Jesus made clear however that receiving a good work for Him is always valid, no matter how extravagant it may appear. Some scholars estimate that the flask of ointment was worth one year's salary. Jesus did not flinch. He made clear that His claim supersedes all others.

We know of course that the person who most complained was Judas Iscariot, the traitor, who spoke out of jealousy and greed, not concern for the poor. He was a thief. Never allow yourself to envy another person's blessing. Rather rejoice that God is no respecter of persons. He also wants to do wonderful things for you. All you have to do is believe and receive.

10

10TH PRINCIPLE

"Take It"

The biblical definition of prosperity or wealth never refers simply to money. Who wants to be rich, but in poor health? Or have a bad marriage? Or have a sick and dying child? No sane person would want these tragedies even if in return it meant all the money in the world. The extraordinary life is not about money. Money is merely a tool. There are far more important issues of life, and you have far more authority over outcomes than you realize. God will give you wisdom, strength and power. He will help you, but You must take authority over the affairs of your life. He will not do it for you while you sit idly by.

You must take control of your life, health, relationships, career and money. Deuteronomy 8:18, which we referred to earlier, says, "And you shall remember the Lord your God, for it is He who gives you power to get wealth, that He may establish His covenant which He swore to your father as it is this day." Notice that God does not give you wealth. He gives you "power" to get it. The word translated "power" is the Hebrew word "kowach" which means, vigor, capacity and substance.

God gives you the spiritual vigor, capacity and substance – the "authority" - to get wealth. He does this to establish His covenant, that is, to prove that He keeps His Word. In a sense then, it is not God who "establishes" or confirms His covenant, but each of us. We establish His covenant by using the power He has given us. He establishes His covenant by delegating power to His people. This is an important distinction which must be understood.

Suppose I told you that I have given you a Rolls Royce. Then I add that it is garaged in California (or on the east coast if you live out west), with instructions by the holder to give it to you when you show up to claim it. I even hand you airline tickets to fly to its location and prepay the shipping costs to have the car shipped to wherever you live. You must simply show up in person to claim it. Others may hear about my promise and say to you that I cannot be trusted. They may even tell you that you must have misunderstood. It is up to you to prove that I am a man of my word by showing up to claim what I promised. It is I who must prove that I keep my word, but unless you act on my word, I cannot prove it. I have given you the "authority" to claim the vehicle, but I cannot claim it for you. You must do that for yourself.

The word for "wealth" in the Hebrew is the word "chayil", which means "force". That force is inward which includes virtue, valor or integrity. It is also outward, which includes money, people and material goods. This should be settled now once and for all: God wants you to prosper. He has given you the claim ticket, but you have to show up.

You have authority. It will not come into your life until you exercise responsibility and lay claim on what God has promised. How does this work? When you put the Word of God in your mouth, you are using the very authority and power of God Himself. His power cannot fail. It is God who gives you His Word, His authority and His Power so that you can confirm His Covenant. God totally identifies with human beings as the crowning glory of His whole creation. He would not have made us in His image and likeness unless He intended us to share in His authority. One of the reasons He gave us His Word is for us to be co-rulers and co-creators with Him.

In a sense you even "co-create" your own salvation. The truth of salvation was already there, created for us by Jesus Christ two thousand years ago when He died on the cross and rose again. Creating the reality of salvation in your own life is your doing. For example, you did not create an airplane, but you create your own flight by taking advantage of that form of transportation. No matter how many airplanes exist, the airline cannot create the fact of you being on a flight. That is something you must create for yourself. Only you have the "authority" to do that.

When God speaks His word, He speaks forth His vision for the way things ought to be. God never had an image of you as destitute, homeless, sick, alcoholic, drug addicted, depressed or in despair. His image of you was one of righteousness, authority, power, glory and prosperity. The image you have and the words you speak should reflect the vision God has for you. Just as your salvation is up to you, your condition in life is up to you. You have the ability, but you must take authority.

Take a fresh look at the Genesis story and you will see God's intention for human beings and the devastating consequences of failing to take the authority He has given us. Remember that everything God spoke into existence came from the image within Himself. This is the "law of Genesis". All created things come from within the creator. You are a creator. What you create comes from within you. You should be diligent about what is inside you because that is the life you are going to create. Proverbs 4:23 says, "Keep your heart with all diligence, For out of it spring the issues of life."

Understand that you are a being created by the Word of God. "...God said, 'Let us make man in Our image according to Our likeness." God spoke words, just as He did with all of creation, but when He spoke of man He spoke words of "likeness" to Him. He also spoke words of authority. "...[L]et them have dominion..." You were made to have dominion over the earth and your circumstances. You were created to dominate, not to be dominated. Just remember that you are to dominate the circumstances and situations of life, not to dominate people.

Not only did God make man from His own image, but He put in man what was in Himself. "And the Lord God...breathed into his nostrils the breath of life; and man become a living being." (Genesis 2:7) God did not breathe oxygen into man. He breathed His Word, His Spirit, wisdom and knowledge into man. He filled you with His own Divine nature. Before man rebelled, he was in complete agreement with God. He was the kindred spirit of His Creator and Father, thinking as God thinks, saying what God says and acting as He acts. This God-like nature was the basis of Adam's authority.

Therefore, when God created these amazing beings He called Adam and Eve, He spoke words of authority to them. "Then God blessed them, and God said to them, 'Be fruitful and multiply, fill the earth and subdue it, have dominion...'" First, He blessed and empowered them. He gave them spiritual power to carry out their responsibilities as rulers of the earth. Then He told them to be creative, that is fruitful. Fruitfulness does not refer to only to procreation. It refers to the creative process itself. God was saying to them, "Expand the beauty and prosperity of the Garden of Eden to the whole world."

He told them to "subdue." The Hebrew word is "kabash," which means "keep under subjection." He commanded them to have dominion, which is authority. The Hebrew word is "radah," which means to "rule and reign over."

God gave the garden of Eden to Adam who was to protect, cultivate and expand it through the exercise of his God-given authority and power. Adam's failure is the "original sin" which brought the fall.

We have said that the word "subdue" in the Hebrew means to "keep under subjection." In a perfect world where there is no sin, why would it be necessary to keep it under subjection? In fact, God's instructions to Adam about caring for the garden held the same warning. "Then the Lord God took the man and put him in the garden to tend and keep it." (Genesis 2:15) "Tend" is the Hebrew word "abad" which means to "work, till or move." To "keep" is the Hebrew word "shamar" which means to "guard" and "protect". What would Adam have to guard against in a world without theft or sin of any kind??

God was warning Adam that there is an enemy who would try to rob him of his authority and put him under subjection. Satan could not take away God's authority, but being cast to the earth, he targeted God's under-ruler: Adam.

The first challenge to the authority of Adam was the tree of the knowledge of good and evil. Jesus told a parable which sheds light on what happened in the garden. "The kingdom of heaven is like a man who sowed good seed in his field;...his enemy came and sowed tares among the wheat...So the servants of the owner came and said to him, 'Sir, did you not sow good seed in your field? How then does it have tares?' He said to them, 'An enemy has done this.'" (Matthew 13:24-28)

I know this is not traditional thinking about the tree of the knowledge of good and evil, but I do not believe God put that tree there. It was the enemy who did this. Think about it. James tells us that God does not tempt any man, and that tree was certainly a temptation. I also believe that God expected Adam to deal with it, even if that meant rooting it out or cutting it down. God never told Adam and Eve they could not touch that tree. He told them they could not eat of its fruit. Eve was the one who said they weren't to touch it, but according to the biblical account, God never spoke to her about it. He spoke only to Adam.

Adam did not have to leave that tree there. He could have removed it. He was given the authority to "move" whatever needed to be moved. God told them they were not to eat of it or they would die. (Genesis 3:4) Adam had the full authority to rip that tree out of His garden. What trees have grown up in your garden which do not belong there? You may be saying, "Why, God, why?" God is saying, "I have given you all the authority and power you need to remove that unwanted growth. Use it!"

Adam did not have to accept Satan's presence in his garden. He was present when Eve was beguiled by Satan and he did nothing. The scripture says, "... [S]he took of its fruit and ate. She also gave to her husband with her, and he ate." (Genesis 3:6) Adam was "with her" when she ate that forbidden fruit. He could have slapped it out of her hand, cast Satan out of the garden, and taken Eve to God for forgiveness.

Even if you believe that God put the tree there and put Satan there, you cannot believe that God expected Adam to stand by idly while Satan beguiled his wife. Would any man reading this watch his wife being seduced and do nothing? No real man would. Adam should have taken authority because God had put him in charge. However, Adam not only witnessed the betrayal and did nothing about it. He joined it by eating the fruit himself.

He committed treason. His was a supreme betrayal of

the Father, who loved him and put everything under him. When he did this, he bowed his knee to a fallen angel - and transferred his authority into the hands of God's enemy. Satan then became the "god" of this world. Satan was telling the truth when he said to Jesus, 'All this authority I will give You, and their glory; for this has been delivered to me, and I give it to whomever I wish. Therefore, if You will worship before me, all will be Yours.'" (Luke 4:5-7) Satan had that authority because it had been surrendered to him by Adam. Had this not been true, there would have been no real temptation What Satan did not realize was that Jesus would soon have all authority in His hands. When He defeated the forces of death, hell and the grave, He rose saying, "All authority has been given to Me in heaven and on earth." (Matthew 28:18) Through Him, that authority has been restored to you, as an heir of God and joint heir with Christ.

The name of Jesus Christ is your authority. God has given Him a name above every name. It is above the names of sickness, poverty, trouble, heartbreak, tragedy and any other evil or negative force which comes against you. Every name must bow to the authority of the name of Jesus. Pray, but do not leave it there. Believe it, see it, speak it, write it, meditate it, take it and receive it. Not only command bad mountains to depart, command good mountains to come. Command trouble to go; peace to come. Command sickness to go; health to come. You can probably think of a thousand different ways to apply this principle. Your life can be extraordinary.

Here are two examples of what you need to be confessing for your financial and physical well being:

"Heavenly Father, You have given me power to get wealth to establish Your covenant. (Deut.8:18) I sow and give in faith, bountifully and cheerfully; I reap bountifully a hundredfold return on my sowing. Lord, You take pleasure in my prosperity and assure that I always have all sufficiency in all things and abundance for every good work (2Cor.9:68); wealth and riches are in my house (Ps. 112:3); all my debts are paid or canceled supernaturally. I owe no man anything but to love him. (Rom.13:8) I put Your Word in my heart and in my mouth, and I make my way prosperous and have good success through the Word of God. (Joshua 1:8) And by the authority You have given me through the Name and Blood of Jesus and the Word of God, I command poverty and lack to go. I command abundance and prosperity to come"

"In the name of Jesus Christ, I declare that I have robust physical health. I bind every sickness and disease of every kind; they will not touch me. Father God, Your Word is in my heart and in my mouth; it is health to all my flesh (Prov.4:22) and strength to my bones (Prov.3:8). You satisfy my mouth with good things, so that my youth is renewed like the eagle's. (Ps. 103:5). I exercise regularly and never eat in unhealthy ways. And by the authority You have given me through the Name of Jesus and the Word of God, physical health is mine in abundance!"

You can also do this with your emotional well being for any challenges which come to you. When you walk by faith and live in the favor of God, you can take authority over every problem and limitation which tries to hold you back.

11

11TH PRINCIPLE

"Never Quit"

One of my concerns in writing this book is that some people might come away with the idea that I am teaching people that they should never have problems. I believe with all my heart that these principles if practiced diligently will help people succeed and overcome obstacles to success, but I do not believe that life can be lived without hardship and pain. You can avoid creating some problems for your self, but you cannot avoid problems any more than you can avoid rain. An umbrella allows you to avoid becoming drenched in the rain, but no one goes through life without getting wet. It is unavoidable.

One of the most important scriptures for any Christian to remember is found in Matthew 7:24-27:

"Therefore whoever hears these sayings of Mine, and does them, I will liken him to a wise man who built his house on the rock: and the rain descended, the floods came, and the winds blew and beat on that house; and it did not fall, for it was founded on the rock. But everyone who hears these sayings of Mine, and does not do them, will be like a foolish man who built his house on the sand:

and the rain descended, the floods came, and the winds blew and beat on that house; and it fell. And great was its fall."

Notice that the same storm attacked both homes. The difference was not in the experience but in the outcome. One man's house stood strong in the face of the violent storm. The other man's house collapsed completely. Trouble comes to the rich and the poor, the educated and the illiterate, to people of every race and background. The difference is how you respond to the challenge. Some fall apart, but eventually find their footing again. Some never recover. You be the person who withstands the assaults of life and continues to fulfill your destiny,

Someone I know had a close friend who died. Several years later, that person was not only still in grief, but suicidal. Every human being who lives long enough will lose loved ones who are part of the very fabric of your life. The only way to avoid that is to die first, not a choice we get to make. The pain of separation from someone you love can seem unbearable. Nevertheless, God will help you recover and go on with your life.

None of the other principles in this book matter if you're going to quit. Once you are clear about your path, pursue it with all your might. It is unrealistic and immature to expect that life will always be easy. You can be doing exactly the right thing in exactly the right way and still face unimaginable obstacles.

For example, I believe that America is a providential nation, ordained by God to be a place of hope, opportunity, prosperity and righteousness not only for our own citizens, but as a symbol to the world. When George Washington volunteered to be Commander in Chief for the Continental Army, he was taking on the greatest challenge of his life. He had to endure humiliating losses, betrayal among his own ranks and extreme deprivation of food, clothing and military supplies. It was a war of endurance and attrition. He lost more battles than he won, but because he endured, he won the ultimate victory. He won our freedom. It was far from easy and it was not pretty, but because he would not quit, he secured the future of the greatest nation to ever exist on the face of the earth.

If you are an American, you are a spiritual and intellectual heir of George Washington. The grit, determination and unswerving commitment to see it through is the stuff of which we are made. Perseverance is in our DNA. We are not quitters. If you are not American, you can still draw inspiration from George Washington and others who endured hardships went on to do great things. Your name may never be written in the history books, but it can be written in the record of heaven that you fought the good fight, finished your course and kept the faith.

When President Barack Obama occupied the White House one of his first acts was to remove the bust of Winston Churchill, which I thought was strangely dismissive of the contribution Mr. Churchill made to freedom-loving people throughout the world. Churchill was one of the greatest figures of the twentieth century. His words are still quoted today as a testament to the human spirit. Germany was armed to the teeth, ready for war and determined to bring England to her knees. One of Churchill's most famous quotes is still used today to remind people that quitting is not an option:

"Even though large tracts of Europe and many old and famous States have fallen or may fall into the grip of the Gestapo and all the odious apparatus of Nazi rule, we shall not flag or fail. We shall go on to the end, we shall fight in France, we shall fight on the seas and oceans, we shall fight with growing confidence and growing strength in the air, we shall defend our Island, whatever the cost may be, we shall fight on the beaches, we shall fight on the landing grounds, we shall fight in the fields and in the streets, we shall fight in the hills; we shall never surrender..."

With those words, Churchill inspired a nation to fight on against impossible odds. With American help, Nazi Germany was defeated and Great Britain was victorious. It took four long years and fifty million dead, but victory was secured. You'll never have to pay that kind of price for your victory in life, but you can be inspired by the knowledge that human beings are capable of achieving the impossible. You cannot be defeated if you will not quit. Never give up.

12

12TH PRINCIPLE

"Always Love"

I am a culture warrior, and have been for over thirty years. I believe that there is only one definition of marriage. It is a union between one man and one woman. God created us and created marriage for us, and it is the height of human arrogance to overturn six thousand years of human history and divine revelation. Not even the Supreme Court has that authority, but some Judges have more than enough hubris.

I believe that there are only two genders - male and female. That's it, and that's all. They are not fluid, and it is not possible except by mental and emotional confusion to move back and forth between the two. There are not 56 genders as Facebook and other institutions of cultural influence would have us believe. All of the cultural craziness we are witnessing is the inevitable result of embracing moral and cultural relativism. The idea that there are no fixed guideposts, no truth to which we are all accountable, leaves human beings to be moral arbiters for themselves, a very dangerous position.

I believe that pre-born children have just as much of a right to live as any one of us. They are human beings and should be accorded the full protection of law. I pray the day will come when we mourn the millions of babies we've allowed to be slaughtered. The scripture is quite clear that God knows and loves that pre-born child, even if its mother and father do not. Psalms 139:13 says, "For You formed my inward parts; You covered me in my mother's womb." Jeremiah 1:5 says, "Before I formed you in the womb I knew you; Before you were born I sanctified you..."

We must continue to persuade our fellow citizens until abortion is eliminated. Planned Parenthood which profits from shedding the blood of these children will one day find themselves on the ash heap of history. It will be relic of an age of spiritual blindness, and we will mourn for the genocidal evil performed year after year. It is my prayer that those who now support it or participate will soon see the light.

Abortion is also propped up by the fallacy of moral and cultural relativism. Forces of the left have largely rejected God and any acceptance of absolute truth. Long held moral standards are altered or dismissed when enough political or legal pressure is applied. Words are completely redefined to serve political interests. This is what the Supreme Court has done in creating a right to abortion and more recently to same-sex marriage.

Five justices invented rights out of their own imaginations because they wanted to and could. They had the power, and they did it. That is the sad truth of the matter. They had neither the Constitution nor morality on their side. Logic and reason were simply camouflage for their personal political and moral perspective. Special interests used political influence to engineer a dramatic rejection of truth, a major cultural shift away from Judeo-Christian values and an unprecedented break with history. The Supreme Court was the tyrannical tool they used to get it done because it could not be achieved by democratic means.

This is the dark road to totalitarianism. For if there is no truth and words mean whatever we want them to mean based on human whim, then might makes right. Truth becomes whatever those with the most power want it to be. Who says it it wrong to steal? It all depends on how you define stealing or who is being stolen from. There have been periods and cultures in history when it was considered virtuous - morally right - for the strong to take from the weak. If "You shall not steal" is not an absolute command from God himself, human beings can and have come to a different conclusion.

Hitler didn't think that confiscating Jewish property was stealing. Communists in Russia, Cuba and Vietnam did not think that taking the property of the wealthy was stealing. Both saw their actions as virtuous, morally right and necessary. Yet they were wrong. They were wrong because the God of heaven, the ultimate moral arbiter, says it is wrong. Therefore, no individual or government has a right to do it, not even under the guise of re-distributive justice. It is still theft. Period.

I want to make clear how strongly I hold these truths, because I want it understood that I feel just as strongly that we must love the people with whom we disagree.

Why should we love people who are fighting against the very principles we hold dear? First, we should love them because God loves them. God loves the homosexual caught up in that lifestyle. He loves the activist who blasphemes God and His word by redefining marriage. He loves the abortionist who makes money off the killing of pre-born babies. He loves the woman who is misled into thinking that killing her child will solve her problems. He loves the thief, the adulterer, the drug dealer, the gang banger and the murderer.

At a left wing women's march held in Washington, D.C., one protester carried a sign which read "If Mary Had an Abortion, We Wouldn't be In This Mess." That is blasphemous and disrespectful, not only of Christianity, but of God Himself. Yet He loves the person who wrote that vile sign. We must find it in our hearts to do so as well. When Jesus hung on the cross, His first words were, "Father forgive them, for they know not what they do."

God's will is salvation, not destruction of those who oppose Him. His heart breaks watching the crowning glory of His creation ignore or defy Him. Yet He loves them because God is love. Of course there are temporal and eternal consequences, but God's predisposition toward man is mercy not judgment. Eternal judgment is the inevitable outcome of a life lived in rebellion against Him, but we should take no joy in their damnation. As much as people may offend or hurt us, we do not rejoice in their fall. Quite the contrary. Second Corinthians 5:11 says, "Knowing, therefore, the terror of the Lord, we persuade men..."

While enemies see our love as a sign of weakness, we know that it is strength. The love of God is not a theoretical idea. It is a reality. If you are His child, born from above, a new creation in Christ Jesus, His love is in you. The love of God has been poured into our hearts by the Holy Spirit. [Romans 5:5] Being like Him is never weak.

There is another reason why you must love people in spite of how much you hate what they do. Anger, bitterness and hatred toward others is unhealthy. It is like poison which enters your system and slowly kills you. All kinds of mental, emotional and physical problems can result from allowing oneself to hate others. The Rev. Martin Luther King said, "let no one make you stoop so low as to hate him." The scripture also warns against it. Hebrews 12:14-15, says "Pursue peace with all people... lest any root of bitterness springing up cause trouble, and by this many become defiled." Pursuing peace does not mean that you can be at peace with everyone all the time. True peace requires the cooperation of all parties. Romans 12:18 warns that peace is not always possible: "If it is possible, as much as depends on you, live peaceably with all men." Some people will not allow you to live peaceably with them, but that does not mean you should hate them.

Let us be clear on what love is and is not. Love means that we do not seek another's destruction, but their highest good. We do not want vengeance against them. We do not rejoice when evil comes upon them. This is a personal ethic and attitude which cannot be applied by society's criminal justice system. For example, when someone commits murder, we do not release him to do more evil.

We incarcerate him to remove him from society to punish and prevent him from hurting others. The criminal justice system cannot say, "We love that person too much to put him in jail." Or, "We know he committed cold blooded murder, but we forgive, and he is free to go." You can personally forgive, but institutions which have the job of protecting the rest of us cannot do that.

The same is true in war. A nation cannot use personal moral ethics in dealing with vicious terrorists who want to enslave or kill us. We must defeat or kill them. However, even in that horrendous situation, we should be motivated by the love we have for those we are protecting, not hatred for those who pose the threat. The enemy may end up dead either way, but it is important that you guard your own heart. A root of bitterness will damage you and those around you. I've heard hatred described as drinking poison to punish an enemy. That's a very accurate depiction of what hatred and bitterness do.

On my twitter account, I was challenged by a follower for my opposition to allowing Muslim refugees from terror racked countries to resettle in America. The person called me unchristian. I tried, albeit unsuccessfully, to explain why you cannot necessarily apply principles of individual ethics to circumstances which require protection of others in your care. The ethic of turning the other cheek does not apply to a situation where someone slaps my wife or accosts my child. Neither does it apply to the protection of the citizens of our country. Our elected leaders first responsibility is to the safety and security of our people. Once that is done, we should help others to the extent we can do so without endangering Americans. Not only is that not unchristian, it is a Christian duty to care for one's own.

As an activist in public policy issues, I draw a distinction between those who are living lifestyles with which I do not agree and their pursuit of public policies to support those lifestyles. I will fight tooth and nail and against those polices, against the "fundamental transformation" of America. However, I will never be disrespectful of others or attack their human dignity.

One of the greatest challenges for someone like me is being true to one's conviction while loving those who hate you and what you represent. I do not claim to have mastered that balance, but I continue to work at it. When I won the Republican nomination for Lt. Governor of Virginia, I faced a media storm for which I was not prepared. They had discovered statements I made in sermons, speeches and interviews on Christian media. Of particular interest to them were my comments about homosexuality. I was asked repeatedly whether I regretted anything I said in the past. My answer then was "no." Today my answer is more nuanced.

I realize now that the way I expressed myself about the LGBT community left me open to the charge that I was hateful and bigoted. Political opponents used and amplified that to convince voters that I was dangerous and wanted to harm members of the gay community. Although that perception was not entirely my fault, I must admit I contributed to it. Instead of merely referring people to the Bible, I often extrapolated in a way that made it seem like personal antipathy. It is difficult to defend a personal opinion that makes others feel condemned.

I should have simply allowed the Bible to speak for itself. It may not be any more appealing to those who disagree, but at least it removes the discussion from the realm of personal attack. Allowing the Word of God to speak elevates the debate to one of religious conscience rather animosity toward others. In the future I will try to remember that distinction and express even to the LGBT community that I can disagree with them and still love them. In fact, I abhor the idea of a person being verbally or physically attacked for their sexual orientation. Not only do I not support such behavior, I oppose it to the point of using violence to defend a gay person if necessary. I will never justify violent or aggressive behavior toward fellow citizens for their sexual orientation or perceived gender identity. Some argue that attacks on people for their sexual orientation are rare. Perhaps they are, but even once is too much.

Some of my friends and supporters were surprised to learn that I actually oppose discrimination against LGBT people in housing and employment, particularly by government. In my view any tax paying citizen should be given fair consideration for employment by government regardless of sexual orientation or gender identity. People have to be able to work and live and have shelter regardless of what I might think of their lifestyle and behavior.

However, I also believe that the First Amendment protects Christians and others of religious conscience from being forced to participate in or provide services for same sex ceremonies or other activities for which they have a sincerely held faith objection. No one should be denied housing or employment, but having a cake baked for a gay wedding is not exactly an essential human right.

Understand that if you are in a situation where your personal convictions clash with the desires of others, do not expect human credit or reward for trying to show love. That has to be something you do because God wants you to do it. He wants to express His love for others through you. You may never get any recognition, particularly from those who view you as the enemy. Do it with the perspective that the eternal rewards are far greater than anything you can hope to gain on earth.

As strongly as I feel about abortion, it is blasphemous that anyone would think that killing an abortionist or bombing an abortion clinic would be right or just in God's eyes. I believe that abortion is evil, but one evil does not justify another. The scripture is very clear. Romans 12:21 says, "Do not be overcome by evil, but overcome evil with good."

No matter how hard it gets, keep loving and forgiving. In doing so you open yourself and others to the love and forgiveness of God, which brings good things into your life and potentially into theirs well. Love is the most powerful force in the universe. "And now abide faith, hope, love, these three; but the greatest of these is love." [1 Corinthians 13:13]

CONCLUSION

"True Success"

Do not overwork to be rich; Because of your own understanding, cease! Will you set your eyes on that which is not? For riches certainly make themselves wings; They fly away like an eagle toward heaven." Proverbs 23:4,5

Everyone wants to succeed. No normal human being wants to fail. Doctors and pharmacists sell millions of pills every year to help people deal with the effects of their pursuit of success. At what price? Addiction? Broken families? Heart attacks? Strokes? High blood pressure? Migraine headaches? Some people literally work themselves to death.

In the 1980's I almost did just that. I graduated from Harvard Law School convinced that the way to success was to work twenty hour days, pushing myself to the physical and mental limit. I was a Christian. I believed in God. I had made Christ the Lord of my life. However, I lacked wisdom. When it came to my pursuit of success and how I would achieve it, I had "a form of Godliness", but was in effect "denying the power thereof." (2 Timothy 3:5).

My law practice was beginning to grow when I took on the additional responsibility of General Manager of a radio station. I had then three full time jobs - attorney, pastor and general manager.

My children missed me, my wife felt ignored, and I was destroying my health.

The first sign that this was no way to live was the onset of massive, debilitating migraine headaches. The word "headache" hardly describes what I went through. They were paralyzing attacks, seizures of pain. There were months when I would suffer an attack every day. Each attack left me immobilized for hours. My answer? Take medication, and stay up later to make up for lost time. Then my blood pressure began to rise, and I needed medication for that. The turning point finally came after one Doctor prescribed a medication for migraines that would thicken the lining of my abdomen and bring on a heart attack if not monitored very carefully.

There I was in my mid-thirties with a full blown health crisis. I looked fine on the outside, but inside I was killing myself, chasing success. I was a born again Christian, filled with the Holy Spirit and living like a fool. It took divine revelation to turn my life around. No matter what I was trying to build, I could not long sustain it on human effort.

When I began to apply the principles of faith outlined in this book and to trust God instead my human effort, the headaches which lasted ten years off and on finally stopped. My blood pressure came back to normal with no medication. I started taking vacations with my family. I eventually stopped practicing law and focused my full attention on ministry. None of this happened overnight. I had to transition from a life spent trying to succeed in the flesh to a life spent functioning in the grace and blessing of God. I have not had a migraine headache or anything close to it in over twenty years.

The reason I've written this book is to help others avoid making my mistakes. Not everyone gets off as easily as I did. My wife and I remain happily married, and I am close to my children. I thank God for His grace.

Some families do not survive what I went through. Some couples suffer painful divorce, and many men end up estranged from or hated by their children. If you are living on your human effort, leaving your family on the sideline while you "succeed," there is a better way. Jesus said, "Come to Me, all you who labor and are heavy laden, and I will give you rest. Take my yoke upon you and learn from Me, for I am gentle and lowly in heart, and you will find rest for your souls. For My yoke is easy and My burden is light." (Matthew 11:28-30)

There will be pressure in life. That is unavoidable. The good news is that you can emerge victorious every time as long as you remember that "...He who is in you is greater than he who is in the world." (1 John 4:4) You can learn to deal with the pressures of life with confidence and calm, grace and peace.

Jesus taught this lesson to His disciples when they were crossing the Sea of Galilee. "And a great windstorm arose, and the waves beat into the boat, so that it was already filling. But He was in the stern, asleep on a pillow. And [His disciples] awoke Him and said to Him, 'Teacher, do you not care that we are perishing?'" The storms of life did not agitate Jesus because he knew that He had authority over them. He "rebuked the wind and said to the sea, 'Peace, be still!' And the wind ceased and there was a great calm."

Jesus did not comfort the disciples in their fear. He rebuked them, saying, "Why are you so fearful? How is it that you have no faith?" (Mark 4:37-40) He had already given them His Word, the word of faith and power. They did not yet know to use it. His disciples could have rebuked that storm, and you can rebuke the storms in your life. I am not talking about weather patterns, but storms of trial and trouble such as financial lack, sickness, marital problems, job layoffs and the like. "Be anxious for nothing, but in everything by prayer and supplication, with thanksgiving, let your requests be made known to God; and the peace of God which surpasses all understanding, will guard your hearts and minds through Christ Jesus." (Philippians 4:6,7) Notice the text says be anxious for "nothing". Anxiety and worry can cure nothing. Whenever you feel the urge to worry, start smiling and laughing, praising and thanking God for the favorable outcome that is already yours. Worry will flee from you.

There was a boy plagued with seizures and suicidal behavior as a result of demon possession. The father of the child took him to Jesus' disciples, but they were unable to heal him. The moment Jesus came on the scene "the spirit convulsed [the boy], and he fell on the ground and wallowed foaming at the mouth." It is interesting that even though Satan is defeated, he puts up a good front. That child was going to be clean. The demon troubling the child knew it, but he tried to intimidate the Master Himself. Jesus rebuked the unclean spirit saying, "Deaf and dumb spirit, I command you, come out of him and enter him no more." That spirit heard the command of faith from the very Son of the Living God, but he still tried to resist before coming out. "Then the spirit cried out, convulsed him greatly, and came out of him." (Mark 9:20-26)

Do not be discouraged by the bullying noises of your circumstances. Your enemies and even well meaning friends will try to convince you that your faith will not work. Ignore them, and press on. No matter what your situation at this moment, you are destined for wonderful things because God loves you. You are blessed beyond measure. Remove from your "garden" the weeds of fear and doubt. Sow in it the flowers of faith, hope and love. You will reap a harvest of good things exceedingly abundantly above all that you've asked or thought. [Ephesians 3:20]

For this is God's will, and this is my prayer for you: "Beloved, I pray that you may prosper in all things and be in health, just as your soul prospers." (3 John 1:2) As good things come to you and you make your life extraordinary, remember to give God the glory.

A personal note: Please write to me and share the stories of your success, and with your permission, I'll be sure to share them with others. A major part of making your own life extraordinary is helping other people to do the same. May God bless you and may you fulfill the unique and extraordinary purpose for which He made you and put you in this place at this time. Now go. Fulfill your destiny, and make your life extraordinary.

E.W. Jackson